The Sugar Bush Connection

Maple Cookery
~"sweet water" folklore
~sugaring off facts
sucré d'érable Recettes délicieuses

compiled at
Cranberrie Cottage, Granville Centre,
Nova Scotia, Canada

by Beatrice Ross Buszek

NIMBUS PUBLISHING LIMITED

The recipes in this book
were hand-lettered by
Beatrice Ross Buszek
at Cranberrie Cottage
in Nova Scotia, Canada

Published by Nimbus Publishing Limited
P.O. Box 9301, Station A
Halifax, Nova Scotia
B3K 5N5

ISBN 0-920852-33-5

First printing 1982
Second printing 1984
Third printing 1988

Printed and bound in Canada by Wm. MacNab & Son Ltd., Halifax, Nova Scotia

Distributed in the United States by Yankee Books, Depot Square, Peterborough,
N.H. 03458

This Collection
of
Recipes and Maple Memorabilia
is dedicated to
the
North American Indians
who
Shared the Sweet Secrets
of the
érable à sucre
with
Early Explorers and Colonists

ACKNOWLEDGEMENTS

Some books owe so much to so many people that it is difficult to make proper acknowledgement. **The Sugar Bush Connection** is such a book.

First I acknowledge all the Maple Sugar growers, women and men from New England west to Minnesota and the Northeastern regions of Canada. They sent me all sorts of information and sketches and pictures — and **recipes**. Special thanks to my daughter Christine who did many of the sketches scattered throughout the book. She-spent most of her younger years in Sugar country — Michigan, Upstate New York and Nova Scotia. The classic **Maple Sugar Book** by Helen and Scott Nearing added to the tone of this book and the bibliography was especially helpful.

The Provincial, State and Federal Departments of Agriculture were enormously helpful, sending me boxes of brochures and folklore and statistics and literature. Similarly, the Maple Sugar Associations were generous and cooperative, people such as Dale McIsaac of Nappan, N.S., Gordon Brookman, International Maple Sugar Institute, Lloyd B. Herman, Turkey Hill *Erabliere*, Brome, Quebec, and Arthur Merle, N.Y. State Maple Sugar Association.

Gage Publishing of Agincourt, Ontario gave permission to quote from **A Concise Dictionary of Canadianisms**, by W.S. Avis et al, and Stephen Greene Press of Brattleboro, Vt. permitted me to use three recipes from **Maple Cooking**, and to quote from **Especially Maine** by Elizabeth Coatsworth. To these and all the others who gave special permissions, many thanks.

Even though it is not possible to incorporate all that I have learned about the secrets of the Sugar Bush and the Maple industry, yet sincere thanks is given to everyone who helped in whatever way to the final version of **The Sugar Bush Connection**.

Recipes from Northeastern Woodlands of North America

entrees

with meat . . .

with vegetables . . .

breads

muffins

make mine Maple

desserts

STUFFED BAKED APPLES ALA SYRUP!

puddings

toppings

A Taste of Maple

How Sweet it is!

cookies

pies

cakes

M · is for maple · · ·
S · is for sugar & sap · · ·

Make ~ Maple Moon Magic

candy

drinks

potpourri

How Sweet it is!

*Don't miss a visit to the
Sugar Bush!*

Kitchen Metrics

Volume
Use metric measures for metric recipes. Measures
are marked in millilitres (mL) and are available in the
following sizes:

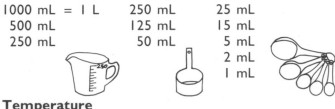

1000 mL = 1 L	250 mL	25 mL
500 mL	125 mL	15 mL
250 mL	50 mL	5 mL
		2 mL
		1 mL

Temperature
Most commonly used oven temperatures

°C replaces °F		°C replaces °F	
100	200	190	375
150	300	200	400
160	325	220	425
180	350	230	450

Refrigerator temperature: 4 °C replaces 40 °F
Freezer temperature: − 18 °C replaces 0 °F

Mass
1 kg (1000 g) is slightly more than 2 pounds
30 g is about 1 ounce

"The maple mark of quality"

ix

PREFACE

What better month than March to begin a new adventure — to bid a "sweet good-bye to winter". The nights are still frosty cold and the warm sun begins to "honeycomb the snow" and the maple moon and the sweet water weather promise that spring is near.

The ambivalent moods of a northeastern winter are forgotten when the warm sap-running winds carry off the patches of old snow; when even the muddy earth becomes a cheery challenge — about mid-March when the Canada geese are heading home. Now there is a sense of a subtle stirring of the spirit, a pervasive restlessness that seems to affect all living things. It is as if the sugar sunshine triggers off an ambrosial nostalgia. We are not immune to the hidden forces that regularly seduce and subdue nature. Robert Frost used to say that "spring is the mischief in me" and the influence of the moon on behaviour is no longer ridiculed by scientists. It is said that in parts of New England even the crows go crazy just before the sap runs!

So — in a very real sense, by the logic of the sun and the moon and the tides, when March comes to the northeastern woodlands of North America, a transmutation takes place. Once again, as if touched by an ancient alchemy, the *Sucrerie* offers its sweetest of gifts and, as if under the same spell, we, too, respond to this renewal of nature. The roots of life go deep and, without our consent, spontaneously with a kind of wonder, we find ourselves responding to spring out of the collective depth within us, as if reaching out for a long lost memory.

March is the sweetest month. With the "salutary sap" of the *érable à sucre*, the season of the hearth comes to a close and the "long sweetenin" days begin,

*And all the time you could see diamond flashes in the woods as a crystal drop of sap caught the sun and glistened for an instant like a sequin. The sap was running.**

Cranberrie Cottage
February, 1982

* Quotation is from J. Jannetti, **The Salt Book**, Anchor Press, 1977, p. 403.

INTRODUCTION

"What is a man but all his connections"
Robert Frost

Being far too typical a consumer of nature's gifts, I knew very little about the secrets of the Sugar Bush until four years ago. Even then the things I learned were mainly by accident while researching and writing THE CRANBERRY CONNECTION and later THE BLUEBERRY CONNECTION. As I came across the many historical references to the *érable à sucre*, I made separate notes, just in case the Maple fever touched me at some later date.

Early last spring I drove on a country road out of Guysborough, Nova Scotia. For miles and miles there was nothing except trees and then, alongside the road, was a Department of Lands and Forests sign. On a sudden impulse I drove down the long rutted road to the Giant Lakes Sugar Woods in the midst of 150 acres of Sugar or Rock Maple trees. The operation is relatively small, only 4000 trees are tapped (40 acres), but I was impressed by the potential Maple Syrup it represented and awed by the grandeur of the isolated Sugar Bush on the headwaters of the Salmon River which empties into Chedabucto Bay.

Then began a period of reading, and writing to the Departments of Agriculture in Nova Scotia, New Brunswick, Ontario and Quebec and the Northeastern States west to Minnesota. This was followed by a more personal letter to the Maple Sugar Associations, requesting snapshots, sketches, anecdotes, personal histories — and recipes — anything that would better acquaint me, and the public, with the past, the present and the future of nature's sweetest industry. I talked with a lot of people and confirmed what I feared was true, that few Nova Scotians or North Americans know much about the secrets of the Sugar Maple. Dorothy Moore from Upstate New York, who, with her husband and two sons has a family Sucrerie on-the-side, wrote me,

You would be surprised at the number of children and adults too, who haven't the slightest idea how real maple syrup is made.

I asked my mother if there was a Sugar Bush near the village where I grew up in Hants County, Nova Scotia. "Oh, no," she replied, "Maple Syrup comes from Vermont or down New Hampshire way." Later I was reminded of one of Haliburton's famous Sam Slick sayings, "Braggin' saves Advertisin' ". With his words ever before me, as well as the words of my mother, ideas for the book began to come together.

The responses to my request soon filled a huge file. A multitude of people I had never met now made a sweet connection with me! This should not have surprised me because the same sort of thing happened during the Cranberry and then the Blueberry adventure. In this increasingly depersonalized world it is a relief to know such people do exist.

The research on the *érable à sucre* began to haunt me. The more I read, the more I re-read — old books, technical journals, and poetry too. It was difficult to focus on recipes when my head was now so full of other wonderings. How could man have so separated himself from nature? I thought of an old poem by Charles G.D. Roberts — so Canadian and yet such a universal plea,

Make thou my vision sane and clear
That I might see what beauty clings
In common forms, and find the soul
Of unregarded things.

Flavoured with such musing, Maple memorabilia, and culinary surprises, the third CONNECTION was soon complete. The pages that follow are some of the things I now know or believe about the *Sucrerie* and the mystery of the sap and the syrup, and some "Braggin' " about the most versatile delicacy in nature, and a collection of sweet concoctions from all over

North America. The recipes range from backwoods to gourmet delights, each one using only pure Maple Syrup or Sugar, except in a few instances where I suggest a few drops of Maple flavouring or extract.

The early calendar began with the vernal equinox in March. When the new calendar was adopted in 1752, the beginning of the New Year was changed from March 25th to January 1st. It is said that the farmers were the most resistant to the change. March seemed a more honest beginning, more accurate, more to the "natural order of things." When civilization was younger, when man lived close to the soil, all living things fit into a pattern — a time and a place and a season. Farming was closely linked to a man's religion and philosophy and the spring of the year had unique significance as a time of spiritual and natural rebirth.

The first crop of the year is the Sugar Bush harvest that begins with the surge of sap that runs each spring for a brief period. Sometimes it starts as early as mid-February and stops as late as mid April. Within that period the heavy sap run may be only ten to twenty days and the flow is directly affected by climatic conditions. The nights must be freezing cold and the daytime sunshine warm. Think on the mystery. Without such precise conditions — 24 °F and 40 °F — the sap will stop running or will not start at all. With all the expertise of the twentieth century, man is still at the mercy of the Sugar Maple magic. All he can do is wait and hope.

The sweet gift of the *Sucrerie* now seems so natural, so much a part of the North American heritage that we take it for granted. Is it not a paradox that the agricultural specialist still regards the conversion of the sap to syrup as one of nature's most intriguing mysteries? An integral part of the

Maple sap enigma is its deceptive taste and appearance — like fresh spring water. Why, then, does the sap take on the distinctive Maple flavour only after it is boiled?

Although the Maple tree can be grown in other areas and is hardy as an ornamental tree or for its hard wood, it requires precise conditions for the sweet Maple magic to repeat itself. Of the thirteen varieties of Maples native to North America, only four produce the sweet sap that makes Maple syrup and only two are heavy producers — the *érable à sucre* or Sugar Maple known also as Hard Maple, Black Maple, Rock Maple, Curly Maple or Bird's Eye Maple (*Acer saccharum Marsh*) and the Red Maple (*Acer rubrum L.*) whose leaf is the emblem of Canada.

The *érable à sucre* does not grow in any quantities outside New Brunswick, Nova Scotia, Southern Ontario and Quebec and the northern States from New England west to Minnesota. Within this concentrated area about 5,000,000 U.S. gallons of pure maple syrup were produced commercially in 1981 of which 3,369,342 were from the Province of Quebec. This does not, of course, include the products of the many family farms that sweeten and colour the northeastern landscape.

With the right weather conditions, the early settlers got sap from other than maple trees. The ash, box elder (Manitoba Maple), walnut and birch can be tapped but the sap will not give the sweet syrup of the *érable à sucre*. In Lady Simcoe's diary (she accompanied her husband from England to Canada in the late 18th century) there is reference to the unique sap of the Maple and that of the birch trees,

> This is the month for making Maple Syrup, a hot sun and frosty nights causing the sap to flow most. Slits are cut in the bark of the trees and wooden troughs set under the tree into which the sap — a clear sweet water — runs. It is collected from a number of trees and boiled in large kettles till it becomes of hard consistence.

*Moderate boiling will make powder sugar but when boiled
long it forms very hard cakes which are better.*

*In a month's time when the best sap is exhausted, an inferior
kind runs of which vinegar is made. Cutting the trees does
not kill them for the same trees bear it for many years
following . . . The sap of the Birch trees will make vinegar.*

York, 19th March, 1794
Public Archives of Canada

The Maple Sugar industry of early days took place in the
yard, in a clearing, in a crude Sugar Shack or in the kitchen. It
was usually the responsibility of the women to supervise the
sugaring-off. Susanna Strickland Moodie who came from
England in 1832 to live in the Canadian wilderness, wrote

*. . . while Jenny was engaged in boiling and gathering the
sap in the bush, I sugared-off the syrup in the house, an
operation watched by the children with intense interest . . . I
was heartily sick of the sugar-making long before the season
was over; however, we were well paid for our troubles.
Beside one hundred and twelve pounds of fine soft sugar, as
good as Muscovado, we had six gallons of molasses, and a
keg containing six gallons of excellent vinegar. (1837)*

Roughing It in the Bush (1852)

Susanna's sister, Catherine Parr Traill, also emigrated to
Canada and she wrote that

*. . . in the backwoods the women do the chief of the sugar
making; it is rough work, and fitted for men, but Canadians
think little of that.*

The Backwoods of Canada (1836)

The word "sugar-off" originally referred to the
conversion of sap to syrup but this colloquialism soon took on
other meanings — the period when the sap is running
(sugaring-off days), the *Sucrerie* as a designated place (the

Sugar-off); a time of merriment that could take a variety of forms (Sugaring-off party or a Sugar-off).

Elizabeth Therese Baird wrote about a Sugar Bush and a Sugar-off on Mackinaw Island, Michigan, in 1802.

A visit to the sugar camp was a great treat to the young folks as well as to the old. In the days I write of, sugar was a scarce article, save in the Northwest, where Maple Sugar was largely manufactured. All who were able possessed a sugar camp. My grandmother had one . . . About the 1st of March nearly half of the inhabitants of our town . . . would move to prepare for the work.

Baird then told of a party "near the close of sugar making". It was a *Crêpe* party. Each woman brought a frying-pan "in which to cook and turn *les crêpes* or pancakes", being first instructed that "no girl was fitted to be married until she could turn a *crêpe*". The food served was not the now typical sugaring-off fare. They ate "partridges roasted on sticks, rabbit and stuffed squirrel, cooked French fashion, and finally as many *crêpes* with (Maple) syrup as we desired". Everyone left the party with a "bark of wax and sugar cakes". (Containers were made of birch-bark and the wax was a soft maple taffy.) The merry-making associated with sugaring-off filled an important need in the life of the early settlers.

Even today the Maple moon means sugaring-off parties. It is a time when families come together — and many tell me they come from great distances — and touch one another's lives again for a brief time in the sweet shadow of a *Sucrerie*; when neighbours gather to celebrate an ancient feast; when communities, even towns, reach out and welcome strangers to the sugar table. In some parts of rural Quebec the sugaring-off season begins with the Blessing of the *Sucrerie* or the Sugar Maple. With the sweet harvest there are sugaring-off parties throughout the Province. Sometimes the celebrations last all night with dancing and food and entertainment for all ages. It is a seasonal festivity and a colourful part of the French-Canadian culture.

From Nova Scotia to Minnesota the Sugar-on-Snow parties are the same but sugaring-off has become big business. For instance, in New England you might be encouraged to send a "really different Christmas gift" — to "Rent Mother Nature — Lease a Sugar Maple Tree or a Sap Bucket for One Year". Or you might be invited to "Visit a Sugar Bush during March and April as guests of sugar makers who cater to Sugar parties". Some Maple producers say "It's awful hard work" to run a *Sucrerie* and a person has to love what he is doing. One writer insisted that "sugarmaking is not for the weak hearted or bodied" as it is one of the "most laborious occupations".

As more and more farms are sold and trees cut down or abandoned and families scattered and young people lured off the land, the old *Sucreries* are disappearing. Progress has taken a sweet toll. When Lawson Smith of Cumberland County, N.S. gave up making sugar, he sold his equipment to other sugarmakers and "the Nova Scotia government bought the land for a picnic park". Smith's grandfather "made sugar back of Stanley" and his three sons bought a 120 acre Sugar Woods in 1894. Ownership changed hands several times and finally in 1932, "the Department of Highways bought the whole lot when they made the highway to Springhill which is now paved." Similar transactions and constant forest depletion have drastically influenced the character of the country and of the people who live there.

This is a time of Maple Renaissance in Canada and the mood extends across the border. The industry is being rejuvenated with continual research and improvement of equipment and marketing skills. More family farms are being reborn as young North Americans recognize and seek the dignity of a simpler life, closer to nature. It may be true as some farmers say, that "it's the worst damn job there is" but when the sap weather winds begin to blow these same farmers can't wait to head for the bush.

*   *   *   *

An introduction to the *érable à sucre* would not be complete without an acknowledgement to the North American Indians who shared the sweet secrets of the Sugar Bush with the early Jesuits and later colonists.

There are many legends, most of which vary only slightly, explaining how the Indians learned to harvest the liquid fruit of the Maple tree and how he discovered the greater mystery of converting this sap to Maple Syrup. Between the recipes that follow are bits and pieces of the folklore and here are a few versions that have survived countless tellings.

The Chief took his tomahawk from the Sugar Maple tree where he had thrown it the night before. As the sun got higher, the sap began to drip from the gash in the tree. The Indian wife tasted it and it wasn't bad so she used it to cook the meat. Or, the pot was left under a broken Sugar Maple branch and the sap dripped into it. Later when the meat was cooked, the sap boiled down to a syrup. The irresistible sweet scent and taste of the maple meat so delighted the Chief that he named it "Sinzibuckwud", the Algonquin word meaning "drawn from trees" and used by the Indian when referring to Maple Syrup.

Visitors to the Sugar Bush, especially those from the towns and cities, are often surprised to know that the Maple Syrup does not flow from the trees in its final thick sweet state. The Chippewas and Ottawas of Michigan believe that many moons ago, the God NenawBozhoo cast a spell on the Sugar Maple tree, turning the near pure syrup into what is now called sap. NenawBozhoo loved his people and feared they would become indolent and destroy themselves if nature's gifts were given too freely. Similarly, another story is that the Earth Mother, Nokomis, made the first Maple Syrup.

She made a hole in the tree and the syrup poured out. Her grandson Manabush was worried. If the sweet gift of the Maple tree was so easily obtained the Indians might become shiftless and lazy. So he showered the top of the Sugar Maple with water, diluting the Maple Syrup into sap. Ever since then it has taken long hard labour to make Maple Syrup.

Marius Barbeau tells us that the Indian gradually reduced the sap to syrup by a series of freezing, discarding the ice and starting again. In the 16th century the Indians had only clay pots in which they boiled meat and fish by constantly adding hot stones to the pot and replacing them with hotter ones. For two hundred years there was no significant change from the methods used by the early Indians. The French Canadians were not interested in the backwoods sugar until imports from France were cut off in the early 1700s, forcing the colonists to be self-sufficient. Similarly, not until the War for Independence in the late 18th century, when sea traffic was blocked off, did the American colonists consider the value of the cruder Maple Syrup. By the end of the 18th century the Maple industry was established in Quebec but mainly as a "typical habitant activity". It was not until the end of the 19th century that iron or tin pots were used to gather and boil the sap, and not until the 20th century has the renaissance of the Sugar Maple industry been taken seriously.

* * * *

As I write the introduction to **The Sugar Bush Connection**, it is early in February, but with each word the winter sunshine seems warmer and the days longer. I fear that a false spring is upon me! Yet this, in itself, is a cue that winter will soon give up, disappearing in puffs of sweet smoke from the *Sucreries*.

Maybe you, too, respond to the season of the sap with its promise of sugar weather and sugar water — the rustic rites of a northeastern spring. Why not make some Maple magic in the kitchen? Or begin Maple sugaring in your own backyard, or tap a few sugar trees in the field of a friendly neighbour. Better still, start a *Sucrerie*. It will mature in forty years and last at least another hundred and fifty — a living legacy of the most versatile luxury of nature. How sweet it is!

Cranberrie Cottage
February, 1982

MICMAC PUDDING

4½ cups milk — 6 Tbsp. corn meal
3 Tbsp. all purpose flour — 1 egg
½ cup each maple syrup and white sugar
2 Tbsp. butter — ½ tsp. salt

Scald 2 cups milk. Combine ½ cup milk (cold) with corn meal and flour. Add to scalded milk and cook until thick. Break egg into bowl and beat, add sugar, syrup, salt, 1 cup cold milk. Add to first mixture, then add 1 cup cold milk. Put in pudding dish, dot with butter, bake at 300° from 1½-2 hrs. Fresh fruit can be added. Serve hot or cold with cream.

FRENCH CANADIAN CUSTARD

2 cups milk — 3 egg yolks
1/3 cup maple syrup — 1 tsp. Vanilla

Lightly beat egg yolks, add syrup
and dash of salt. Stir into scalded
milk. Cook in double boiler till
mixture adheres to the spoon. Add
Vanilla. Chill well before serving.

In the spring of the year
"the Indians came down from
Manitoulin to sell their maple
sugar... in mackinaws, open
boats with a schooner rig;
and the sugar was carried
in mocooks ... made of birch
bark, which hold from twenty
to thirty pounds."

The Pioneers of Old Ontario
1923

2

An old Maple tree has
the sweetest sap...

CREAMY MAPLE

3 cups brown sugar – 1/3 cup maple syrup
1/3 cup milk – 2 Tbsp. butter – salt
1/2 tsp. each nutmeats and vanilla

Combine all except nuts and vanilla.
Stir gently - low heat- until dissolved.
To not stir but boil to soft ball
stage. Cool. Beat until thick and
creamy. Add flavouring and nuts.
Grease pan and cut before mixture
hardens.

MARITIME TOPPING

6 large marshmallows
1 egg white — dash of salt
½ cup maple syrup

Cut marshmallows into small quarters. Beat egg white until slightly stiff. Bring syrup to boil, then add marshmallows and salt and blend well. Pour over egg white and beat until well blended. Chill. Versatile. Pour over desserts, cakes, pudding, ice cream.
Makes 1½ cups.

MAPLE APPLE SAUCE

Cover with boiling water, 4 large apples,
pared, cored and cut in quarters.
Add 2 whole cloves. Cook until done
and put through a sieve. Return
to heat, adding 1 Tbsp. vinegar
and 3/4 cup maple syrup. Cook
about 10 minutes. Beat in
1 tsp. butter.
Can be served hot or cold. It is
especially good with roast pork.

NEW ENGLAND GINGERBREAD

¾ cup maple syrup — ½ cup butter
½ cup brown sugar — ¼ cup milk
1 tsp. each soda and ginger
2 cups sifted flour — 1 T. water

Sift ginger and flour. Add soda
to the Tablespoon of warm water.
Beat egg and add sugar and
butter. Add soda water to the
maple syrup and stir into the
egg mixture. Add milk. Stir in
flour until well mixed. Bake
in buttered pan at 375° for
about 30 minutes.

"Blessed of the Lord be
his land... for the precious
things put forth by the
moon, and for the chief
things of the ancient
mountains, and for the
precious things of the
lasting hills."
Deuteronomy 33:14-15

6

Cole Bowman, an artist from Elmira, Ontario, sent me this print and the one used for the cover. He wrote, "please feel free to use for whatever you wish and good-luck."

7

Down East Cracker Pie

Roll out about ¾ cup fine crackers
1 cup maple syrup — 1 cup water
½ cup each — butter, vinegar, white sugar
Raisins and assorted spices

Combine in saucepan and cook a
few minutes, then bake in a two-
crust pie. Bake at 400° for 10 mins,
reduce to 350° for 20-30 minutes.
(Makes 2 pies)

By the early 1800s sugar was
a regular part of the diet
because the tea and coffee
habit had started.

North Country Cookies

1 cup maple sugar — 3½ cups flour
1 tsp. baking powder — ½ cup butter
2 eggs — ¼ tsp. salt

Cream sugar and butter, add eggs
and beat. Add dry ingredients.
Roll, chill and slice. Bake at
150° F about 12 minutes.

MAPLE CHIFFON PIE

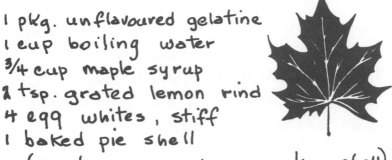

1 pkg. unflavoured gelatine
1 cup boiling water
¾ cup maple syrup
2 tsp. grated lemon rind
4 egg whites, stiff
1 baked pie shell
   (pastry or graham cracker shell)

Dissolve gelatine in water and stir.
Add maple syrup and lemon rind.
Cool. Beat egg whites until stiff
and fold two mixtures together,
continuing to beat until fluffy.
Turn into pie shell. Chill.

"The lips of my charmer are
sweet as a hogshead of maple
molasses."
       thomas Fessenden 1806

MAPLE FRUIT BLOSSOMS

1 cup maple syrup — 2 egg whites
1/3 cup seedless raisins
1/3 cup candied lemon peel
1/3 cup chopped figs (optional)
1 cup broken walnuts

Measure syrup into large saucepan. Boil to 254°F - until soft
ball forms when dropped into
cool water. Beat egg whites
until stiff. Add syrup slowly.
Beat until mixture peaked. Fold
in fruit and nuts. Drop by
Teaspoonfuls about 1" apart, on
waxed paper and leave overnight.
(or use lightly greased baking
sheet). Bake in very slow oven
(200°F) for 1 hour. Makes
about 36 meringues.

"the sound of the whip-poor-will
was a harbinger of spring and
a warning that the time to
cease sugar-making had arrived."
Eliz. therese Baird, 1802

GREYWOOD FUDGE

2 cups each maple syrup and white sugar
1 cup raisins — 2 stiffly beaten
1 cup nutmeats   egg whites

Boil syrup and sugar until it forms a thread. Gently add to the beaten egg whites. Continue to beat, adding raisins and nuts. Cool in a pan and cut into small squares.

"The splendid sap of the Maple tree is better than any lemon or cherry water, or any other drink, none of which has such an exquisite taste nor is it so healthy. but few people bother about making any, nobody cares for things that are ordinary; children alone, so to speak, take the trouble to tap those Trees."

Nouveaux Voyages, Vol. II
Baron de Lahontan 1700

Marc Lescarbot said that if
the Indians "are pressed by
thirst, they get juice from trees
and distil a sweet and very
agreeable liquid, which I have
tasted several times."

Histoire de la Nouvelle France, 1609

CANADIAN CAKE

Combine softened ½ cup shortening
with 1 cup maple syrup. Add to
this 1 cup unsweetened thick
apple sauce.
Thoroughly flour about 1 cup
chopped raisins. Mix together
2 cups sifted flour — ½ tsp. salt
½ tsp. each cinnamon and cloves
¼ tsp. nutmeg — 1 tsp. soda

Gradually add dry mixture to
first mixture, then fold in the
floured raisins. This makes
a stiff batter. Just before
baked (¾ to 1 hour) sprinkle with
grated maple sugar.

12

SPRING TONIC

¼ cup maple syrup — ¼ cup lime juice
1 cup light rum — 1 cup gingerale

Combine and stir well. Use a shaker or blend well. Pour over crushed ice to serve.

"The first run, (of sap) like first love, is always the best, always the fullest, always the sweetest."

John Burroughs
Winter Sunshine 1881

13

"In 1848 nearly four million pounds of maple sugar was manufactured in Upper Canada."

Weekly Globe, 16 Nov 1849

MAPLE TEA
(Serve hot or cold)

6 cups orange-spice tea - <u>strong</u>
1 cup maple syrup ⌐ ½ c. orange juice
¼ cup lemon juice

Combine. Stir well to dissolve the maple syrup. Chill well before serving.

To serve hot, it is best to heat in a double boiler so it will not boil. (Should it boil, it will take on a bitter taste).

Makes about seven mugs.

The Maple Tree –

"a standing
miracle of
goodness"

Quebec Whipped Cream

3/4 cup whipping cream
1/4 cup MAPLE SYRUP

Thoroughly chill the cream and the
syrup. Then beat cream until
begins to thicken. Add syrup, a
small amount at a time, beating
constantly, until stiff peaks.

Makes about 2 cups. Use as
topping or filling — the possibilities
are endless — the effect is
fantastic.

DETROIT SPARERIBS

3 lb. spareribs — 1 cup Maple Syrup
1 Tbsp. each Worcestershire sauce,
   chili sauce and vinegar
1 small onion, finely chopped - salt
¼ tsp. dry mustard - ⅛ tsp. pepper

Roast ribs on a rack at 220°C
(425°F) for 30 mins. Drain fat
from pan. Cut ribs into serving
pieces. Place in 9 x 13 - inch pan.
Combine remaining ingredients in
saucepan. Boil 5 mins. Pour over
ribs in pan. Bake, uncovered, at
190°C. (375°F) for 1 hour. Baste
and then turn ribs over after
one hour. To serve, skim fat
off remaining sauce and serve
with the ribs.   4 servings.

Classic fare for an
evening meal - especially
during a winter blizzard -
is pancakes drenched in
pure maple syrup.

The woods, the lakes and rivers, contain food of different descriptions. If the moose, deer and rabbit, the salmon and the trout, gaspereaux, herring and shad, supply the wants and necessities of the wandering tribe of Indians, without one artificial product of the land, it must be acknowledged that it is not the fault of the country, if a settler cannot make a comfortable living, who, besides these advantages, possesses the means of cultivating a luxuriant soil. To the new settler the sugar maple-tree is very valuable. In the early part of the spring of the year, when the first sap rises, the tree is tapped, and a certain quantity of the sap or juice drawn off, which is then boiled down, and manufactured into sugar. In some parts of the country, large quantities are made, and in most of the families on new farms, a sufficiency for their own consumption. The process is attended with very little labour, and one tree will yield annually from five to eight pounds. In the United States, they know better how to appreciate the advantage of this tree than the inhabitants of Nova Scotia. Some years ago, in two towns in Vermont, containing no more than forty families, 13,000 weight of maple sugar was made. In some parts of that State the inhabitants are beginning to line the roads with maple trees, and it would certainly be very advantageous to Nova Scotia, if its farmers would adopt the same practice. The granulation of the sugar is easily performed and the quantity, colour, and flavour of it, when well made, is equal to any sugar manufactured in the West Indies.

Thomas Chandler Haliburton
A GENERAL DESCRIPTION OF NOVA SCOTIA
Halifax, 1825

SUGAR GLAZE

Thoroughly mix together ½ cup sugar, ½ cup maple syrup and about ¼ cup water in a small saucepan. Quickly bring to a boil, then reduce heat and simmer about 3 minutes. Remove from heat.

Beat into the mixture ⅓ cup confectioners sugar, until smooth. Spread while hot.

(If glaze is used on cookies or squares, store them in layers separated by wax paper. They will keep for 2 or 3 weeks in a tightly sealed container).

¾ cup of Maple syrup equals 1 cup sugar. If substituting reduce liquid by 3 tablespoons for each cup of syrup used.

"... an ancient wooden shack among magnificent old Maple trees... the steam from the boiling sap was pouring out through every crack."

MAPLE GLAZE

½ cup butter, heated until golden brown. Gently blend in 2 cups Confectioners' sugar and 2 tsp. maple flavouring. Icing should spread easily so you can add 2-4 Tbsp. hot water if needed.

When the maple syrup is cooked to candy, the French-Canadians call this la tire, or "the pull." They pull the candy into ropes before it hardens.

MICHIGAN MAPLE PIE

Make a 1-9" pie shell of your favourite pastry.

Gently heat 1½ cups Maple Syrup until ½ tsp. soda is dissolved. Do not bring to a boil. When it is cooled, pour into the pastry shell.

Combine 1 cup sifted flour, 1 cup brown sugar, ½ cup butter.

When well blended, spread over top of maple syrup. Bake about 30 minutes at 350° F. Watch it — put a foil sheet underneath as it tends to boil over. (Not for Weight Watchers)

MAPLE COFFEE CAKE

Soften 2 pkgs. yeast in ½ c. warm water
Combine:
½ c. shortening — 6 Tbsp. sugar
3 tsp. salt — 1 c. scalded milk

Stir in 4 eggs and softened yeast.
Gradually add 6½-7 cups flour.
Beat well after each addition.
Knead. Cover and let rise.
Divide into 6 parts. Roll each into
a rectangle about 8x12. Spread
with MAPLE FILLING (p. 142,143).
Roll up and place in pan, or pie
plate. Cut slits in top of roll.
Let rise and bake at 350° about
30 minutes.
For a change, make only 4 rectangles
and make 1½ times the filling

"A Blessing on your basket
and your Kneading Trough."
Deuteronomy 28:5

A history of Michigan Maple has been printed. Write to Michigan State Univ. Ext., E. Lansing, Mich.

MAPLE MELON

Scoop out a Honey dew melon into balls. Soak melon balls in maple syrup and rum mixture and serve on lime sherbert.

MAPLE CORNFLAKES

3/4 cup maple syrup — 1/4 cup butter
1/2 cup cornflakes — 4 Tbsp. cocoa
5 Tbsp. milk — Vanilla

Melt butter and syrup, add milk, vanilla and cocoa. Fold into corn-flakes. Put in small heaps. Do not bake.

Maple butter should be tightly covered to prevent drying, or covered with a thin layer of water.

LOYALIST BROWN BREAD

½ cup maple syrup — 1 cup corn meal
2 cups Graham flour — 1 cup sour milk
1 tsp. soda — pinch of salt

Combine. Bake in medium oven at
about 375°F for 1 hour. If batter
is too heavy, add milk, a drop at
a time.

The measure of a Sugar Bush
is not the number of trees, but
the number of buckets that can
be hung. (Be sure to wait
until the trees are mature
before you tap them.)

Cumberland County Cake

Boil gently 1¼ cup maple syrup
Beat 2 egg whites well.
Beat 2 egg yolks, add ½ tsp. Vanilla
Add yolks to maple syrup.
Gently fold the two mixtures together.

Sift together and fold into above
mixture:
  1 cup flour — ⅛ tsp. ground
  1 tsp. baking powder   (Coriander
  Dash of salt

I like to make this cake in a
Bundt pan. Bake about 1 hour
at 325°F.   Cool at least on
hour on a rack, then remove
from pan.

Top with sprinkled confectioners
sugar or your favourite icing.

Vermont was the first State
in the Union to have a man-
datory Maple Syrup grading
law.

24

"These trees are ... rock or sugar maple, and in the back settlements have great value in furnishing a luxury which the young settlers would otherwise be unable to procure."

Letters to Nova Scotia
Moorsom, 1830

PICTOU PUDDING

1 cup flour - 1 cup brown sugar
2 Tbsp. butter — 1 tsp. cinnamon
1 tsp. baking powder — 3/4 cup milk
1 cup nut meats — 1 cup raisins
Dash of salt — Maple Syrup

Combine butter and sugar. Slowly add milk and dry ingredients alternately. Gently fold in nuts and raisins. Pour into greased 13 x 9 x 2 - inch baking pan. Cover generously with MAPLE SYRUP. Bake for 35 mins. at 375° F. Serve with whipped or plain cream.

25

MAPLE BUTTER SPREAD

Use only first quality fresh syrup. Heat syrup above boiling point of water. Remove immediately. Pour boiling syrup to a depth of only 1½" in a well-chilled flat pan. Cool pan quickly to 50°F. With two wooden paddles, quite like those used for making creamery butter — about 3" wide — scrape the thick syrup from one to the other. Allow about 2 hours to produce the maple butter. Store in a cold place.

Maple Syrup Production:

67 Nova Scotia maple operations produced 65,130 litres of syrup from 157,000 taps in 1983. Note this figure is up from 54,250 litres in '82 from 139,700 taps.

The sugar maple is not found in Europe except as an ornament.

MAPLE ICING
½ cup maple syrup ~ 1 egg white

Beat egg white well. Gradually add maple syrup, continue to beat until icing peaks.
Should cover a 7"x 7" cake.
Serve immediately or keep cool as icing is uncooked.

"The manufacture and use of Maple Sugar was expected to provide a material part of the general happiness which heaven seems to have prepared for mankind."
1791

27

— Sugar Devil —
"for drilling"

PINEAPPLE - MAPLE PUNCH

3 qts. pineapple juice - unsweetened
1½ cups lemon juice — ⅓ cup lime juice
3 cups orange juice — 1 cup sugar
1½ cups maple syrup

Combine and chill, mixing thoroughly.
When time to serve, pour over
ice in punch bowl. Gently add
4 - 28 oz. bottles ginger ale and
2 - 28 oz. carbonated water - bottle
should be pre-chilled. About 75 cups

Before 1790 maple sugar was
rarely used as a staple along
the Saint Lawrence river, except
by the sugar-makers.
    Maple Sugar: Its Native Origin
    Marius Barbeau, 1946

Friday, March 20, 1981   THE CHRONICLE-HERALD   THE MAIL-STAR   3-M

This sketch of Maple Sugaring
in Nova Scotia is not the
usual style of the artist,
Bob Chambers, a native of
Wolfville, whose clever
and amusing cartoons in
the Halifax Chronicle and
later the Chronicle-Herald
delighted Nova Scotians
for over half a century.

MAPLE FRIED SWEETS

Heat fat for deep-frying, about
375°. Beat together until stiff:

    3 egg yolks - 1 egg - ½ tsp. salt

Gently add:

¼ cup Confectioner's sugar

1½ Tbsp. maple syrup

Measure 1 cup flour and add all
at once. Knead well, using floured
surface. Make into two balls,
rolling each one out nearly paper
thin. Cut into shape of diamonds
making a slit in each one at one
end. Draw tail of diamond thru
the slit, curling back in opposite
direction. Fry in deep hot fat -
Turn quickly when lightly browned.
(about 30 sec.) Drain on towelling
and sprinkle lightly with Confectioner's sugar.

In Japan, about 30 % of the
deciduous forest are varieties
of Maple.

30

MAPLE PFEFFERNÜSSE

¾ cup light brown sugar — ½ cup butter
1 egg — ½ cup maple syrup
3⅓ cups flour — ½ tsp. soda
¼ tsp. salt — ½ tsp. clove
½ tsp. cinnamon

"The maple mark of quality

Mix butter (shortening can be used)
sugar, egg, maple syrup and
about 3 drops of anise oil
mixed with 1 Tbsp. of hot water.
Sift flour and blend dry ingredients. Knead dough gently until
pliable for shaping. Mold into
wee balls — 1 inch in diameter —
and bake about 12 minutes on a
greased sheet.
These cookies will harden so it is
suggested that they be stored with
a slice of apple.

Mix a Maple Special: Add at least
3 tsp. pure Maple Syrup to your
favourite fizz: Bacardi, Sour,
Old Fashioned or other drink.

31

... he is the third generation of a family that has made sugar every spring for seventy years ... he knows by trial with ladle when the syrup "aprons off" or "hairs off."

MAPLE FRIED APPLES

Cut cooking apples into ½ inch slices and fry in hot lard or bacon fat. When golden brown, turn and fry other side. When tender, drizzle generously with maple syrup and serve at once.

... we brought in pails and pans of snow to "sugar off" ... by the steaming pans, there was mighty joking and story telling.

MAPLE CINNAMON TOAST

Cream together enough butter and maple syrup to cover required number of slices. Spread on the toast and sprinkle top with cinnamon. Serve immediately

Baked Fresh Fruit
(with Maple)

Place peeled and halved fruit in
shallow pan. Cover with syrup
(4 large pears or peaches need
about ½ - ¾ cup MAPLE SYRUP)
Bake at 350° F until tender.
Serve hot or cold with whipped
cream, or plain cream or blend.
Lovely with Raspberries, blueberries
and wild blackberries.

Frozen Maple Mousse

Lightly beat 4 egg yolks
Beat 4 egg whites very stiff
Combine the yolks with
1 cup Maple Syrup and cook
in double boiler until thick.
When cool, add the stiff
egg whites to which 2 cups
of whipped cream are added.
FREEZE

HINT: If recipe says 2 cups of
sugar and you want to use
maple sugar - use 1 cup sugar,
1¼ cups maple syrup and use
½ cup less liquid than recipe
calls for.

This recipe reminds me of the
words of Ralph Waldo Emerson -
"Thou art to me a delicious torment"!

CORNELL TOPPING

¼ cup maple syrup — 3 egg yolks
1 Tbsp. lemon juice — ½ c. heavy cream
— dash of salt —

When maple syrup starts to boil,
remove from heat and cool.
Add the well beaten egg yolks.
Heat only 1 minute. Cool.
Add lemon juice and salt. Just
before serving, whip the cream
and fold it with the maple mixture.

French Toast with Maple

6 to 8 slices of bread — 5 eggs
½ cup Maple Syrup — 1 cup milk
¼ cup light cream — salt, nutmeg

Beat eggs with Maple Syrup. Add
milk, cream, salt and nutmeg.
Dip bread, one slice at a time,
then drain and fry in a hot
buttered pan on both sides.

"Pastry Impressions"

Maple Mousse

Heat 1 cup Maple Syrup at low
heat. Beat egg whites (2 eggs)
until stiff. Add syrup mixture
to egg whites. Serve in small
dessert dishes, garnished with
flaked almonds, grated coconut or nuts.

There are times when I still feel an alien to country life. But one of the best things about Cranberrie Cottage never changes — my neighbors! Each season, with its unique problems, I am again reminded how fortunate I am — securing a mailbox in cement by the highway; draining the pipes when the little house is alone and powerless in a winter storm; clearing the snow, pulling me out of the mud or leaving a load of cow manure; bringing oil at dawn on a frozen Sunday; calling on the phone just to say she misses the lights in my house when I'm away ... So many such things would fill another book.

———→

My wine-making neighbor promises to help me clear brush around some old maples on the lot-line. Then I'll tap my first tree. Such fun!

John and his wife, Jessie, drink the sap as a refreshing tonic. But they use the sap to make Wine du Maple too. Here is a recipe to try some Indian spirits from maple nectar:

ALGONQUIN AMBROSIA

1 gallon Maple Sap (or water) - 3 lemons
¼ gallon Maple Syrup - 1 pkg. wine yeast
¼ tsp. Grape Tannin - Yeast nutrient

Peel lemons, remove pith, boil peel - 15 mins. Strain, add water to 1 gallon. Add lemon juice, nutrient, tannin and Maple syrup. When syrup dissolves, about 70°F, add yeast. When fermentation slows - about 1 week - syphon into gallon carboy and airlock. When wine clears, rack into clean carboy and leave until all fermentation finished.

Bottle - be patient - for at least three months!

PAIN PERDU (French Toast)

6 thick slices French bread - (day-old)
1¼ cups milk — ½ cup Maple syrup
2 eggs, beaten — ½ tsp. Vanilla
Flour — clarified butter for frying
Crumbled maple sugar for serving
or drizzle with maple syrup

Optional: 2 Tbsp. Grand Marnier

Heat milk slightly - do not boil -
so maple syrup will blend well.
Add vanilla and Grand Marnier.
Soak bread in this mixture.

Now dip each slice into the
beaten eggs, then quickly
into flour. Shake off excess
flour and fry in butter
until golden, slightly crisp, on
each side. Turn once.
Sprinkle with maple sugar or
Syrup and serve hot.

ANNAPOLIS VALLEY SPECIAL

Using double-boiler, cook ¼ cup rice with 2 cups milk and ½ tsp. salt. Prepare six apples – pare, core and cut in halves crosswise. Cook apples until barely tender in 1¼ cup maple syrup mixed with 1 cup water.

Add rice and apples alternately with apples on top. If any syrup mixture remains, pour it over the top layer. Fill cavities of top apples with maple syrup, and crushed nutmeats well mixed. Can be served with cream.

41

42

SUGAR-ON-SNOW

This is the heart of the famed "Sugaring-off" party:

Boil the maple syrup. Most versions suggest 230-250°F. on the candy thermometer. If you have no thermometer, drop a Tablespoon over some hard-packed fresh snow (usually the snow is served in small dishes or even plastic coated plates for a large party). The maple syrup is transformed on contact with the cold snow. Suddenly before you is a waxy, sweet, chewy taffy-like concoction, the like of which you can't quite describe — but every year when the sap weather comes, there is a yearning for one more taste of this—nature's sweetest mystery.

Most recipes suggest old-fashioned pickles in brine as a side dish.—and doughnuts.

SPICY MAPLE BREAD
(recipe makes two loaves)

3 cups sifted pastry flour
1 cup boiling water — 1 egg
1 cup maple syrup — 2 tsp. soda
½ cup brown sugar — ½ tsp. salt
½ cup shortening — (mix with pork
     or chicken fat if available)
1 tsp. each cinnamon and ginger
½ tsp. each cloves and nutmeg

Mix flour, salt, soda and spices.
Cream sugar and shortening, adding
maple syrup into which the beaten
egg has been stirred. Gently stir
in all dry ingredients, and slowly
add the boiling water.

Butter and flour two pans and
pre heat oven to 350°. Bake
about a half hour. Serve with
a hard sauce or whipped
cream topped with slivered
almonds and sprinkled with
nutmeg.

Broiled Curried Scallops

2 lbs. scallops — ¼ cup maple syrup
¼ cup prepared mustard — 1 tsp. lemon juice
2 tsps. curry powder

Line broiler pan with foil and
arrange scallops. Combine the
syrup, mustard, lemon juice and
curry powder. Using half the
mixture, brush scallops - broil at
lowest level 10 mins. Turn scallops,
brush with remainder of mixture.
Broil 10 mins. Serves 5 or 6.

MAPLE SPICE COOKIES

1. Sift together on wax paper:
   3½ cups all purpose flour
   ½ tsp. each baking soda and cinnamon
   ¼ tsp. each gr. cloves and gr. Cardamon
   ¼ tsp. ground ginger

2. Beat well in a large bowl:
   1 cup honey ~ 1 cup maple syrup
   1 egg ~ 2 Tbsp. orange juice

3. Blend above into flour mixture. Add
   4 ozs. finely chopped candied orange peel
   ⅓ cup finely chopped almonds
   Dough should be stiff and sticky.
   Wrap in wax paper. Chill overnight

4. Divide dough into quarters. Roll
   out ⅛-inch thick on floured
   board. Use a cookie cutter -
   about 2½ inch size. Keep about
   1-inch apart on greased sheet.
   Bake 400° for about 8 minutes.
   Cool on racks.

5. While still hot, brush top with
   hot SUGAR GLAZE. (See p. 18)

TURKEY HILL RED CABBAGE

1 Red Cabbage - medium size
1½ tsp. salt - ¼ tsp. pepper
⅛ tsp. nutmeg (freshly grated
                 is preferable)
3 Tbsp. Vinegar
2 large cooking apples
3 Tbsp. MAPLE SYRUP

Quarter and core the washed
cabbage. Cut into slender strips.
Season with salt, pepper, nutmeg
and vinegar. Mix well. Place
in well buttered casserole.
Bake approximately 45 minutes
at about 350°- a moderate oven.

Peel, core and slice apples. Stir
into the cabbage after adding
the MAPLE SYRUP. Cook about
30 minutes more. Serve from
oven to table.

from Turkey Hill Erablière
Brome, Que.

BAKED HAM SLICE

1 ham slice, about 1" thick
½ cup granulated maple sugar
1 cup orange juice — 1 tsp. cornstarch
⅛ tsp. ground ginger

Preheat oven to 325°. Combine
maple sugar, cornstarch and
ginger in shallow baking dish.
Stir in orange juice.
Add ham slice - coating well
on both sides. Bake 45-60 mins.
basting with the sauce.

"It is perhaps in the kitchen that one is most aware of the human past, for the kitchen... was the center of existence of the farm."   Henry Beston
Especially Maine

PARRSBORO PIE

Begin with a one-crust shell using your own recipe. Do not bake.

2 cups maple syrup — ½ cup br. sugar
1 cup flour — ½ cup butter — ½ tsp. soda

Pour syrup into shell after adding soda to it. Combine sugar, flour and butter. Sprinkle over syrup. Bake about ½ hr. at 350 F.

Catharine Parr Traill objected to hanging fat over the boiling syrup, "a common plan but I think by no means a nice one."
The Canadian Settlers Guide
1860

MAPLE BISCUIT ROLL

Use your favourite baking powder biscuit recipe. Roll into a thin dough, slice tart apples and spread over the dough. Roll and slice.

In a saucepan combine 2 cups maple syrup, 1 Tbsp. butter and 2 cups hot water. Bring this to a boil. Add slices (you may want to put mixture in a baking dish.) and cook at 400°F until golden brown. Serve with the hot sauce spread over the top.

Pasture land first reverts to berries, then such trees as ash, birch and poplar – then the softwoods – then the Maples.

It takes a pile of wood 8'x 4'x 4' to boil 250 gallons of sap into 5 gallons of syrup. Another pile half as big is used to turn the syrup into hard brown sugar.

pour un soir d'hiver

Côtelettes de porc sauce aigre douce   (OR)

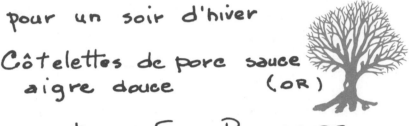

Sweet and Sour PORK CHOPS

4 thick pork chops
¾ cup Tomato Juice ~ 1 Tbsp. Vinegar
¼ cup MAPLE SYRUP - ½ tsp. dry mustard
¼ tsp. ground cloves - Small bay leaf
Salt and Pepper

Brown chops in dab of fat. Add salt and pepper and place in 2 quart casserole. Combine remaining ingredients - bring to a boil. Pour over chops. Cover and bake (350°) about 1-1½ hours.

from Turkey Hill Erablière, Brome, Quebec

An efficient Sugar House
should hold at least two
cords of dry cordwood.

VERMONT ROLLS

2 Tbsp. shortening — 1 c. scalded milk
1 Tbsp. sugar — 1 yeast cake
½ tsp. salt — 2½ c. flour

Mix and raise about an hour. Roll
out on lightly floured board and
sprinkle with broken pecans and
dribbles of maple syrup. Dough
should be about ½" thick. Roll
dough and slice in about 1-inch
pieces. Place each one in a
muffin tin on top of a few nuts
and 1 Tbsp. maple syrup. Let
the dough rise and then bake
at 400°F for about 20 minutes.

Maple syrup is the first
crop of the year.

BACKWOODS ROLY POLY

Prepare biscuit dough rolled out to
½ inch thickness. Brush with
melted butter and top with peeled,
cored, sliced apples mixed with
maple sugar and nutmeg. Roll
like a jelly roll Place in shallow
dish, cover and steam 1½ to 2 hrs.
Uncover, sprinkle lightly with
grated maple sugar and serve
plain, or with Hard Sauce.

Maple Sugar is a North
American product. In order of
output - Quebec, Vermont, New York,
Ohio, Michigan, Pennsylvania and
New Hampshire. (95% of the
Maple Sugar and 80% of the syrup)

53

MAPLE Apple FRITTERS

Make a drop batter and beat:
1 Tbsp. maple sugar ~ 1⅓ cup flour
2 tsp. baking powder ~ ⅔ cup milk
1 egg, beaten ~ pinch of salt

Slice, pare and core required number of apples. Make slices about ¼ inch thick. Dip each slice in the batter and drop into hot fat, as with doughnuts. When lightly browned, remove to drain on heavy brown paper or several layers of paper towels. Serve at once with maple syrup drizzled over the top.

"Honey is found in the trees and is gathered amongst briar and bramble bushes." 1521

"Often the sweet water, freezing in the trough at night, cracked it asunder and made it useless."

Edmond Savoie

MAPLE SYRUP BRITTLE

2 cups maple syrup — dash salt
2 Tbsp. butter — 1/4 tsp. cream Tartar

Combine in saucepan and boil to 280°F. To prevent sugar crystals, do not stir syrup. Pour into lightly greased 7" x 7" pan, being careful to avoid scrapings from saucepan. When firm enough, mark into squares. When cold, invert pan and top gently on bottom to remove candy. Break into "brittle" squares.

GLENGARRY SWEET BREAD

2¼ cups flour — ¾ cup brown sugar
1¼ tsp. salt — ¾ tsp. baking soda
1 tsp. double-acting baking powder
⅓ cup shortening — 2 eggs, beaten
½ cup milk — ⅓ cup maple syrup
2 tsp. grated lemon peel

Grease and flour 3 loaf tins - or
one 9 x 5 loaf pan. Preheat oven to
350°F. Combine first five ingredients.
Cut in shortening.
In a small bowl combine beaten eggs,
milk, syrup and lemon peel. Mix well.
Stir the two mixtures together until
flour is moistened. Spoon batter
into pans.
Bake until toothpick comes out dry.
Cool on racks 10-minutes, then
remove from pans and cool more.

Loaves can be frozen.

"The Beauce is probably the best
maple syrup district in Canada
and undoubtedly has the best
sugaring-off parties."

ST. ANN'S SPECIAL

Toast six slices whole wheat
bread on top of stove- toast
only one side. Butter the other
side. Sprinkle over the butter-
1½ cups maple sugar, crushed
and rolled. Place on a cookie
sheet under the broiler until
sugar has melted.
The toasted maple is lovely served
in a bowl with whipped cream.

The weather controls the
sap and the Sugaring. "Sugar
makers feel the sugar weather
in their bones." Scott Nearing

COLLECTING MAPLE SAP.
PARRSBORO N.S.

Maple hasti-notes were
designed by Alice Ferguson
and her brother, David McCrine
of Parrsboro, N.S. The
designs are based on
a visit to K. Davison's
Sugar Bush about
8 miles from Parrsboro
at Halfway River.
It is a "hobby farm"
in the midst of beautiful Sugar Country

The Indians mixed "ground corn
with chestnuts, beans and berries",
sweetened with "sugar from the
maple tree."

Indians sprinkled maple sugar
over fish boiled in water, substituting the sweet for the salt.

"Many a farmer sits up all night boiling the sap... and a lonely vigil it is amid the silent Trees."
John Burroughs
Signs and Seasons 1914

SUGAR WOODS PARRSBORO, NS

COLLECTING SAP BY PIPELINE, PARRSBORO, NS

BUTTER ICING from Upstate — with Maple Syrup

6 Tbsp. butter — 6 Tbsp Maple Syrup
2 cups confectioners sugar
½ cup chopped nut meats

Cream butter and beat into syrup. Add sugar gradually. Beat until smooth.
Will ice a double-layer cake - sprinkle with nuts.

Maple sugar making in the bush.

TONGUE WITH SWEET-SOUR SAUCE

4 lbs. beef tongue — ½ cup vinegar
½ cup maple syrup — ½ cup boiling water
1 chicken bouillon cube — 2 tsp. whole cloves
⅔ cup seedless raisins — 1 small lemon
(thinly sliced)

Boil tongue gently in salted water
until tender, 3 - 4 hours. Drain.
Remove skin and roots and place in
baking pan. Combine remaining
ingredients and pour over tongue.
Bake at 375° for 45 minutes, basting
frequently. Remove meat to
serving dish, slice it, remove the
cloves from sauce and spoon over
slices. Serves 6 to 8

from <u>Maple Cooking</u> ©1969, Beatrice Vaughan
Rep. by permission The Stephen Greene Press,
Brattleboro, Vermont.

Sap spiles are made from
the Staghorn sumac tree.
Do not confuse this with the
white or "poison sumac."

61

ACADIAN NAVETS

Peel and slice about 1½ pounds young turnips. Saute in saucepan with about 2 Table-spoons butter. Sprinkle with 1 Tablespoon maple sugar. Cook until golden brown. Add ½ cup boiling water with 1 bouillon cube dissolved in it. Cook until tender.

The CREE Indians called the Sugar maple, SISIBASKWATATTIK, (meaning TREE).
The OJIBWAY called maple sugar, NINAUTIK, (our own tree).

Herodotus called sugar, "manu-factured honey."

"When carefully made, this sugar is very sweet... and it is wholesome for the stomach... It's preparation, besides, involves almost no cost... but the people really do not make enough for exportation, and in this they may be wrong. There are many other things in this country that are likewise neglected."

Journal d'un Voyage
Charlevoix, 1744

MAPLE BANANA EGGNOG

Peel 1 banana and cut into small pieces. Either with a beater or in a blender, combine with 1 egg, 2 Tbsp. maple syrup, 1 cup COLD MILK. Makes 2 drinks - but makes you want 3!

Some secrets from the Sugar Bush Kitchens~

▶Maple syrup is 64 % carbohydrates compared to 100 % in granulated sugar ...

▶1½ lbs. maple syrup gives 10 % of daily amount of iron required by a physically active person ...

▶Maple Syrup keeps indefinitely in a freezer. Keep opened containers cold to better maintain the delicate maple flavor...

▶If you wish to put your syrup into several smaller containers, heat syrup to 180° F. Fill hot sterilized jars - leave no air space Seal and place in boiling water for ten minutes ...

▶1 gallon pure Maple Syrup weighs 11 pounds ...

▶Sugar content of sap averages 2.5 % and sugar content of syrup is 66 % or more...

▶A maple tree is about 40 yrs. old or more before it is tapped ...

MAPLE TURKEY GLAZE

About 1 hour before turkey is cooked, remove from oven. Take bird from roasting pan and place in a heavy-duty foil lined shallow pan. Cover with 1 3/4 cups maple syrup and return to oven. Cook 1 hour more, basting about every 15 minutes.

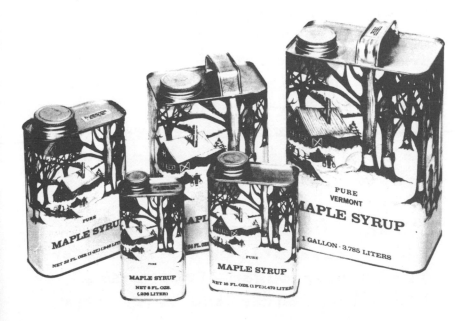

MAPLE FILLED COOKIES

1 cup maple syrup — 1 cup shortening
3 beaten eggs — 1½ cups brown sugar
3 tsp. soda — 2 tsp. cream of Tartar
6 cups flour — 1 Tbsp. vinegar
1 tsp. salt — ½ tsp. all spice
½ tsp. cloves — 1 tsp. cassia

Sift 5 cups flour with spices and
salt. Combine in another bowl
sugar, maple syrup, eggs and
melted shortening. Add soda
and cream of tartar dissolved
in the vinegar. Stir in the
flour, salt and spices. Add
remaining flour if needed to
make a medium stiff dough.
Roll very thin and cut.

Filling: Cook together until thick.
2 lbs. ground crackers — ⅔ c. water
⅔ c. brown sugar — 1 cup raisins.
Add 1 Tbsp. butter and ½ tsp. maple
extract or 1 Tbsp. maple syrup.
Filling goes between two cookies, on
buttered sheet. Bake 12 mins. at 375°.

Maple Museum in Spring

MAPLE SQUASH MUFFINS

½ cup maple syrup - ¾ cup milk
¼ cup sugar — 1 Tbsp. soft butter
2½ cups sifted flour — dash of salt
1½ tsp. baking powder — 1 cup squash
1 tsp. cream of tartar — ¼ tsp. soda

Preheat oven to 400°. Combine dry
ingredients, to which milk and soda
are gently added. Mix squash,
butter, sugar and syrup. Combine
everything and stir, but only
until everything equally damp.
Butter a dozen muffin tins. Bake
about 20 minutes.
(Zuccini can be substituted
for the squash — or even pumpkin)

67

MAPLE MERINGUES

½ cup maple sugar — ⅓ cup butter
1 egg yolk   — 2 Tbsp. milk
1 ¼ cups flour   — ½ tsp. baking powder
¼ cup citron, chopped fine
¼ cup candied ginger, chopped fine
Maple meringue

Cream sugar and butter. Stir in egg yolk and milk. Measure the flour and add floured citron and ginger to butter mixture. Add 1 cup plus 2 Tbsp. butter and baking powder. Blend and chill.

Preheat oven to 350°. On lightly floured board roll out dough ⅛" thick. Cut out with your favourite cutter. Place about 1" apart on greased cooky sheet. Top with 1 tsp. Maple Meringue. Bake 10-12 mins.
Makes about 5 dozen sweets.
(See page 139 for Maple Meringue)

COLLINGWOOD MUFFINS

Preheat oven to 400°.
Sift together:
2 cups flour — ¼ cup sugar
3½ tsp. baking powder — ½ tsp. salt
Combine and add to above:
1 beaten egg — 1 cup milk
¼ cup vegetable oil (or shortening)
Stir — but batter should be lumpy.

Fill greased muffin tin ⅓ full.
Top with 1 tsp. of MAPLE BUTTER.
Fill tin to ⅔ full, using more
batter on top of MAPLE BUTTER.

Bake 20-25 mins. Serve hot.

MINCE MEAT VARIATION

1½ lbs. boiled bottom of round - chopped.
Chopped apples - 3 times more than meat
Skins, chopped fine, of 2 oranges
Juice of 2 lemons and 4 oranges
¾ lb. chopped citron — 3 Tbsp. salt
1 pkg. each currants and seeded raisins
2 Tbsp. cinnamon — 1 quart cider
1 Tbsp. each of nutmeg, clove, ginger
2 cups maple syrup.

Combine chopped meat and apples
Add juice of lemons and oranges,
chopped orange skins, citron, raisins,
currants, spices, salt and cider.
Mix well and add maple syrup.

Simmer in large pot until
apples are soft.

A variation is to add brandy
to the mincemeat mixture
before storing.

70

KEENE PIE

Make your favourite pastry for a two-crust pie.
Slice apples very fine and fill pan. Sprinkle generously with maple sugar. Cover with three or four very thin slices of salt pork (I had difficulty believing this too!) Cover with top crust. Bake about 40 minutes at 350°.

A variation is to lightly butter (or use lard or shortening) top of crust and sprinkle with flour, but lightly wash off excess flour, giving crust a flaky look. (Yes, it sounds wierd but when I received this recipe, I tried it to be sure it wasn't a joke. It is super!)

SPRING DELIGHT

Beat 3 egg whites until stiff
Cook 3/4 cup maple syrup until it
threads. Combine with egg whites
and continue to beat. Fold in
whipped cream _ amount
depends on how you intend
to serve this. I usually use
1½ to 2 cups whipped cream.

Pour into freezing tray and
do not attempt to stir again
before serving.

SUNDAY TOPPING

Using double boiler, combine and
cook 2 Tbsp. sugar, 1 egg white,
1 cup maple syrup, salt, and
⅛ tsp. cream of tartar, over
boiling water. When beaten stiff,
frost top and sides of cake.
Cover topping with slivers of
toasted almonds.

Story is told of Indians at
Pidgeon Lake hiring iron kettles
in 1835:

As soon as the sap begins to rise,
the squaws betake themselves in
families ...to maple groves or sugar
bushes... There they erect a camp,
and prepare troughs, and firewood
and collect all the kettles they can
borrow or hire ... they begin to tap
the trees with a Tomahawk ... the
younger ladies ... collect the sap
and bring it to the fire ... the most
experienced ...(regulates) the heat

❋❋❋❋❋❋❋

Photograph on Page 73
    From The Lens of Lyon
                Howard and Ruth Lyon
                1781 Slaterville Road
                Ithaca, N.Y.   14850
On the Sugar Bush of
    Dorothy and George Moore
    Freeville, N.Y. 13068
("The tree takes 10 or 11 sap pails")

74

"Sweet Water" brewed from nature has been the invention of poets and writers for thousands of years. As long ago as 40 B.C., Virgil's dream of the Golden Age depicted a sweet syrup emerging from the forest trees.

MAPLE TAPIOCA PUDDING

Soak 1/4 cup Tapioca in 1 cup milk overnight. Combine with 3 cups milk and scald.

Combine and add to hot milk mixture:
4 Tbsp. corn meal — 1 cup maple syrup
1 egg — 1 tsp. each ginger and salt
1/2 tsp. cinnamon

When mixture begins to thicken, place in buttered baking pan. Bake at 325°F about 1 hour. Remove and stir in about 1 cup half and half milk/cream. Reduce oven to 275° and bake about two more hours.

Sprinkle with chocolate or serve with hard sauce.

Maple Hints

Add some maple syrup to mashed turnip, along with butter and seasoning.

Add 2 Tbsp. maple syrup to a glass of cold milk. Shake well.

Add maple syrup to commercial marshmallow cream for a special sundae sauce.

Add 2 Tbsp. maple syrup with salt and pepper to cavity of baked Acorn squash.

PARFAIT AU SIROP D'ERABLE
(looks good - tastes good)

1 cup MAPLE SYRUP ~ 3 egg yolks
3 egg whites ~ 2 cups whipped cream
Sliced strawberries, (raspberries or
    blueberries left whole)
white Rum

Heat MAPLE SYRUP in double
boiler. Beat egg yolks well and
add to syrup - slowly - stirring
constantly. When slightly
thickened, cool. Beat egg whites
until stiff, add whipped cream.
Place in a soufflé dish and
refrigerate several hours. Garnish
with berries and sprinkle well
with white RUM.

Turkey Hill Erablière,
Brome, Quebec

MAPLE SYRUP

77

SUGAR PARTY
(for 24-34 people)

1 gallon Pure Maple Syrup
1 bushel of clean snow - from
   under new fallen snow +
3 dozen unsweetened doughnuts,
   preferably raised
1 quart of sour pickles and
   delived eggs, milk, coffee, etc.

+No snow? Buy shaved ice. Snow
will keep unmelted for hours in
a sealed carton.

MAPLE SUGAR FUDGE
2 cups MAPLE SUGAR - ½ pint cream

Combine in saucepan and boil to
240° F. (soft ball in cool water)
Remove and cool to lukewarm.
Beat until mixtures appearance
is dull - not glossy. Pour into
buttered pan - 8"×4" loaf pan -
and cut before fudge hardens.

MAPLETON BAKED BEANS

2 cups dry beans — 6 cups water
3 inches stick cinnamon — 1½ tsp. salt
⅓ cup maple sugar (or dark brown)
¼ cup vinegar — 4 Tbsp. maple syrup

Wash and dry the beans. Cover
with cold water, bring to boil and
simmer about 4 minutes. Cover,
remove from heat about 1 hour.
Add cinnamon and salt. Cover and
simmer 2 hours, or until tender,
adding water if necessary.
Stir in the maple sugar and vinegar.
Remove cover and cook about
a half hour. Add maple syrup.

GRAND-PÈRES
(dumplings cooked in maple syrup)

2 cups MAPLE SYRUP — ¼ cup milk
1½ cups flour — 2 tsp. baking powder
2½ Tbsp. butter — ½ cup water

Combine dry ingredients and cut
in butter, then add the milk. Stir
well. Add water to the maple
syrup and bring to boil in a deep
pot. Drop batter in syrup - as
large as you wish — then cover,
turn down heat slightly and
simmer. Dumplings usually take
15 minutes, depending on size.
They should be dry inside.
Before serving, cool slightly.

There are many versions of the
grand-pères because in French
Canada, the fin becs (gourmets)
are every where. Some of the
best food in the world comes
out of the French Canadian
tradition.

The quality of sap is determined
by weather, shallow tap holes, poor
crowns, dirty equipment, carless
collecting.

JOHNNYCAKES with MAPLE

2 cups corn meal — 2 Tbsp. maple sugar
2 tsp. salt — 2 cups milk

Combine and stir until all lumps are
gone. Grease pan with butter or
bacon fat. When hot, pour the
mixture, a Tablespoon at a time
and cook until edges are crusty.
Turn quickly. Keep griddle well
greased and hot.

Serve the cakes hot with
maple syrup that has been
heated (but not boiled.)

"May it long be the mission of the
Maple thus to sweeten the cup of
life."

Robert Frost said that his farm
in Franconia, N.H. was "backed up
to the foot of Sugar Hill."

SHERBROOKE SHERBET

2 cups MAPLE SYRUP — ½ pint cream
Yolks of 2 eggs — beaten until fluffy
Finely chopped almonds

Boil syrup at high speed for
about 5-7 minutes. Beat in the
fluffy egg yolks. Add the cream,
still beating the mixture. Add the
almonds. Chill. Then freeze
overnight.

"Captain Shaw has given me
a tea-chest in bird's-eye Maple.
It is beautiful wood, the
colour of satten wood."

Diary of Lady Simcoe
26 April, 1793

MAPLE SYRUP FUDGE

2 cups MAPLE SYRUP — 4 Tbsp. butter

Combine in large saucepan and boil to 234°F. (should hold together when dropped into tap water). Remove from heat and cool slightly. Beat until mixture begins to lose its gloss. Pour into buttered 8" x 4" loaf pan. Before completely hard, cut into squares.

Jean and Leslie Grue in Bass River, N.S. tell a familiar story. Most of their syrup is sold to friends and at the Glooscap Co. Bazaar in Economy, and to the family.

Jeans tells of her father who would whittle wooden spiles in the long winter evenings. The Grues made wax, cream sugar and maple butter. They put a piece of pork rind over the boiling syrup so it would not run over.

"sucre d'erable" (maple sugar)
in France is synonymous with
Canada. The Sugar Maple cannot
adapt itself to foreign surround-
ings and remain productive.

Marius Barbeau

BASS RIVER FUDGE
Bring to a boil 2 cups maple syrup,
¾ cup wayo cream or blend and
2 Tbsp. butter. Boil uncovered until
a drop in cold water forms a soft
ball. Cool but do not stir. Then
beat until creamy, turn into a
buttered pan. Cut in squares.

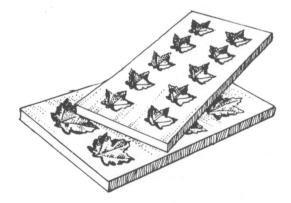

March is the sweet seasonal gap when winter and summer overlap...

MARCH FUDGE

2 cups sugar — 2½ cups maple syrup
1 14½ oz. can evaporated milk
1 cup butter — 1 cup broken nuts
1 12-oz. pkg. semisweet chocolate
1 7-oz. jar marshmallow crème
1 tsp. vanilla (or maple flavouring)

Combine sugar, syrup, milk and butter in buttered 3-qt. saucepan. Cook slowly to soft ball stage. Remove from heat, adding the chocolate pieces, marshmallow creme, nuts and flavouring. Beat well until blended. Pour into well-buttered pan - 13x9x2-inch. While still warm, make squares and cut when cool and firm.

Climb a MAPLE Mountain!

"Henries squaw and family came from the Sugar Bush. They say the Maples give no more water."
1804

ERABLIÈRE COOKIES

1 cup flour
½ cup maple syrup
½ cup butter (or shortening)
1 cup chopped pecans
⅔ cup light brown sugar

Sift flour and nuts. Combine and bring to a boil the maple syrup, butter and sugar. Stir constantly. Remove from heat and gently -- add flour and nuts.

Drop batter about 3" apart on greased cooky sheet. Bake about 5 minutes. Let stand out of oven about 5 minutes. These should be lovely to look at and sweet, sweet to taste.

MAPLE REFRIGERATOR COOKIES

1 cup shortening — 1 egg, beaten
3/4 cup. brown sugar (or maple)
2 Tbsp. maple syrup — 3 c. flour
1½ tsp. baking powder — ½ tsp. salt

Cream shortening and sugar.
Add beaten egg & syrup, sifted
flour, baking powder & salt. Mix
well. Shape into 2 - 2" rolls. Wrap
in waxed paper. Chill until
firm. Slice ⅛" thick. Place on
greased baking sheet. Bake
in hot oven — 400°F - about
8 minutes.

"... a wild delicacy of flavor that no
other sweet can match... It is
then, indeed, the distilled essence
of the tree."
John Burroughs
1886

87

MAPLE CRUMB PUDDING

Pour 2 cups hot milk over
   1 cup soft bread crumbs
When crumbs are very soft, add
  1 slightly beaten egg or 2 yolks.
To this add 1/3 tsp. salt and
    1/3 cup grated maple sugar
Then add 1/2 cup broken walnuts
   and 1 1/2 tsp. melted butter
Put into greased baking dish,
  set dish in pan of hot water
  and bake at 325° until set –
  so when a knife inserted in the
  centre comes out clean.
Serve warm or cold – with cream.

"The sugar-man wears many hats.
He is weatherman and woodcutter,
Trail-blazer and tree expert, trans-
porter, pipe-fitter, cook and chemist,
demonstrator, processor, packager
and retail merchant.
        Pioneer Valley Assoc.
        Northampton, Mass.

— Sugar Devil —
"for drilling"

The Maple Sugar got so hard a special tool was designed to break it.

APRICOT MAPLE SOUFFLE

Put 3 Tbsp. apricot jam through a sieve, adding 1 generous Tablespoon maple syrup. Whisk 3 egg whites very stiff. Mix gently. Bake in cool oven for 20-30 minutes. Serve at once.

When a crow caws on a Hillside, it is spring. Winter is over... time to get the rusty spiles and sap buckets down from the beams in the woodshed. It is Maple Syrup time.

Then it is that the party lines go humming mad... Sap's runnin'! Runnin'! Runnin'! It's runnin' good.

89

Some excerpts from
<u>Maple Sugar Making</u>
by Lawson Smith, Nappan,
Cumberland Co., N.S.

"In the early days all maples
were tapped by an axe cut,
any break in the bark will
allow the sap to run. Squirrels
cut off the bud end of a limb
to get the sap."

"The cream sugar had a method
of its own. Cooked to about
238°F. then cooled to ice cold,
warmed to loosen from the sides
of the pot and beaten to turn
white, Tricky, will set in pot
sometimes before you can put
it in the moulds."

1910 prices:
Sugar and Candy   .15¢ a lb.
Syrup   1.00 gallon
Higgs - Maple Cream   .20 - .25¢ a lb.

"The horse and sled, with enough cans for that road, were breaking the sled road, while we were breaking the path for sap gathering. The first two men with no load broke the path for the last man with the cans. This worked quite well if one of the first men didn't wander off to find spruce gum."

Ephraim Smith said that the Ripley Bros. of Fenwick, Cumberland Co., N.S. were still using birch bark containers in 1894 to catch sap in. A small birch bark container was used to hold maple candy (wax), that was first cooled by being spread on snow and then gathered up and broke in pieces."

"To peel this birch bark was a big undertaking, the full moon in July was considered the best time... Also in July was a good time for black flies. They would be waiting for you by the dozens, with their aunts, uncles and cousins."

"The sap was gathered in wooden tubs placed on a sled hauled by horses or oxen". Some had "four of these tubs that held about 20 gallons each" or "one big wooden tub that held about 100 gallons "

"In the early days the maple producers got a better return, more sap and sweeter." The maple trees were in their prime-age and storms slow them up. "One sleet storm alone... set the trees back forever."

"Like cows, some trees under the same conditions are better than others."

"Boiling water or sap will scald, but boiling syrup will cook you because it has more heat. Even a splatter on hands or face will cause pain.

Ernest E. Coates of Nappan sent me a copy of Lawson Smith's sugar story.

92

Writers have delighted in the imagery of the word "Sugar Off". Archibald MacMechan (<u>Headwaters of Canadian Literature</u>) wrote that one day on a Windsor stage coach, Judge Thos. Chandler Haliburton overheard a fellow passenger talking to a country woman. She was talking about a Temperance speaker and she used the word "Sugar Off". The story is that Haliburton got his material for his famous Sam Slick stories from just such moments and he quickly took out his note book and jotted down "the racy phrase."

94

The Algonquin Indians called maple sugar, "Sinzibuckwud." Can you pronounce it? I can't.

FOAMY FROSTING

1 cup maple syrup — 1/3 cup sugar
2 egg whites, beaten — slivered almonds

Cook syrup and sugar together until it forms a thread. Pour syrup slowly over egg whites. Beat until will hold peaks. Gently fold in slivered almonds.

"I have never seen a reason why every farmer should not have a sugar orchard, as well as an apple orchard."
Thomas Jefferson, 1808

95

OHIO BAKED BEANS

2 cups yellow-eye beans — 2 tsp. salt
½ lb. salt pork with rind scored
½ tsp. soda — ¼ tsp. dry mustard
½ cup MAPLE SYRUP

Soak picked-over beans overnight.
Then boil about 20 mins. in salted
water, adding soda the last five
minutes. Drain.
Place half of salt pork in bottom of
bean pot. Add beans with MAPLE
SYRUP and mustard. On top place
the half of salt pork, scored rind
up. Cover with boiling water.
Bake about 6 hours, covered, at
325° F. Add water if necessary.
Uncover and cook one more hour.
Serves six huge helpings.

Although the sap of the Maple can
provide a "spirit", the Nearings
hoped "this precious gift will never
be prostituted... to this ignoble purpose."
1950

96

MAPLE-ORANGE CHOP SAUCE

Use your favourite stuffing for
6 pork chops, 1" thick.
Sauté chops with butter over a
low heat — about 6 minutes each
side. Add 1 cup maple syrup mixed
with ½ cup orange juice to skillet.
Cover and simmer 20 mins. Remove
cover — cook 15 mins. more, basting
frequently.

Some maple sugaring tricks are older than Canada... then there is— finally, the clear, golden-brown goodness, the essential sweetness of the Mickton tree, the stuff the redmen believed to be "the blood of the Manitou, the great god of the forest."

Kenneth MacNeill Wells

MONCTON MOUSSE

1 envelope unflavoured gelatine
1/4 cup cold water ⌐ 3 eggs
1 cup MAPLE SYRUP ⌐ 1/2 pint whipped cream ⌐ 1 Tbsp. grated chocolate

Soften gelatine in cold water 5 mins. Beat maple syrup and yolks in a double boiler. Cook and stir 10 mins. Add gelatine. Cool but do not set. Beat cream until peaked – add, with whipped cream, the maple syrup. Beat egg whites & fold into maple mixture. Refrigerate. Garnish with chocolate.

MAPLE SUNSET

2 cups cranberry juice - chilled
2 cups light cream - chilled
1 cup maple syrup

Combine. Stir well to dissolve
syrup. Chill well and serve
over ice. Makes 4 generous mugs.

"The fire is kept bright all day and night. Two women are detailed to watch the kettles closely, for when the sap boils nearly to syrup, it is liable to bubble over at any moment... they use a branch of hemlock and dip it in quickly."

Eliz. therese Baird

BOSTON BAKED BEANS

1 quart parboiled red kidney beans
1 cup MAPLE SYRUP ⏤ ¼ lb. salt pork
¼ cup chili sauce ⏤ 1 small onion
⅛ tsp. pepper ⏤ ¼ tsy. dry mustard
1 tsp. ginger ⏤ dash of salt

Score salt pork and add to about half of the beans. Mix half of the MAPLE SYRUP and other ingredients and combine with all the beans in a bean crock. Cover with boiling water and bake at 300° for 4 hours. Uncover, add rest of MAPLE SYRUP and bake another hour, adding water if necessary. Serves at least six helpings.

Peanut Butter Maple Fudge

½ cup maple syrup — ½ cup milk
1 cup brown sugar — ½ tsp Vanilla
1 cup white sugar — Pinch of Salt
¼ cup corn syrup — ½ cup peanut
      butter — smooth or chunky

Combine and cook all except
butter and vanilla — medium heat.
Boil to 238° on candy thermometer.
Add Peanut Butter and Vanilla.
Beat until smooth. Pour into a
buttered pan.

"A sap-run is the sweet
good-bye of winter... the
fruit of the equal marriage
of the sun and frost."
        John Burroughs

"Three copious meals ... are daily
served up ... maple molasses, pease-
pudding, gingerbread, and sour
crout."

Canadian Scenery I
1840

ALGONQUIN SAUSAGE

Cover a 1 lb. link of skinless
sausage with a small amount of
water. Cook for 10 minutes at
325°. Remove from oven, pour
maple syrup over the sausage.
Cover sausage and bake until
tender. Just before serving, remove
cover and brown the meat.

Maple Syrup adds to the taste
of Polish sausage - cut into
2" chunks and simmered in the
syrup.

FOX - RIVER HAM

Bake ham until about a half hour before done. Brush liberally with a mixture of orange marmalade and maple syrup. Experiment a bit with the amount of maple syrup. You might want to add some extra syrup on top of the mixture.

Question: What was origin of the term, "the innocent Maple" and what approximate date?

Answer:
In the late 18th century, strong voices against slavery began to be heard in the colonies. In an 1842 HISTORY OF VERMONT, the Maple Sugar was praised, "it is never tinctured with the sweat, and the groans, and the tears, and the blood of the poor slave." People were asked to support the "innocent maple" and not cane sugar!

MAPLE BLUEBERRY MUFFINS

⅓ cup Wheat Germ — ½ tsp. salt
1 ¾ cup all-purpose flour — 1 egg
⅓ cup maple sugar — 1 cup milk
1 Tbsp. baking powder — ¼ cup oil
1½ tsp. grated lemon rind
1 cup fresh or frozen Blueberries
(well drained)

Combine flour, wheat germ, sugar,
baking powder, lemon rind and
salt. Blend thoroughly.
Beat in small bowl, egg, oil and
milk. Add liquid ingredients to
first mixture. Barely stir.
Fold in Blueberries.
Fill muffin paper cups ⅔ full
(grease well if muffin Tin used)
Bake 25 minutes at 400° F.
Sprinkle top of warm muffins
with grated maple sugar.

The harvest of sap suitable for
maple syrup ends when the tree
begins to bud.

Sugar Bush Relish

Clean, core and chop about
6 lbs. of firm tart apples.
Mix together:
1 pound raisins — 2 oranges (juice
                  and grated rind)
3 cups sugar — 1¼ cups maple syrup

Cook slowly — about 1 hour, stirring
frequently. About 5 minutes before
removing from heat, add ½ pound
shelled broken walnuts. Use at
once or store in sterilized glasses.

NORTHFIELD COOKIES

1 cup maple syrup ⌐ ½ cup butter
1 tsp. soda ⌐ 2¼ cups flour
1 tsp. salt ⌐ 1¾ tsp. baking powder
1½ tsp maple flavouring

Bring syrup to a boil. Remove
from heat. Add soda and butter.
Blend remaining ingredients
except maple flavouring and
stir well. Chill slightly. ~~Add~~
flavouring.
Preheat oven to 350°. Roll out
paper thin dough using scant
flour on board. Cut as desired.
Bake on lightly greased sheet
about 6 minutes. Watch! Do not
bake too long.

Green is said to be the
colour of Hope. Green
is the colour of Spring,
a time of promise

The Sugar Maple is self-supporting,
self-seeding and self-perpetuating.

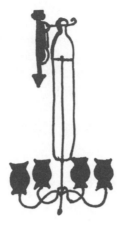

"There is a human and poetic
quality in maples, which is easily
felt, and though the land would
be worth more for its lumber
than for its sugar, many farmers
would no more part with their
maple bush or orchard than
with any precious heirloom."

"The Green Mountains in Sugar Time"
        Harpers, April, 1881

On that first night of "boiling" the sugar maker's family will sit down around the kitchen table for a little well deserved rest and josh each other about their recent sap gathering experiences in the sugar bush. It doesn't matter now that the sap had once frozen solid in the buckets and that a spooked deer had crashed through the new fangled pipe line, for here comes Mother setting out the sauce dishes full of the first taste of syrup, to be enjoyed of course, with a fresh batch of donuts. *"By Gory, after all is said and done, sugaring is fun!"*

MAPLE APPLES

¾ cup maple syrup ~ ¾ cup white sugar
½ cup warm water ~ 10 red firm apples

Combine syrup, sugar and water and stir until dissolved. Cook over low heat until syrup is brittle when a drop is tested in cold water. Put saucepan over warm water. Insert skewers in apples, plunge them into the hot syrup and twirl until apples well covered. Stand in a tin or jar until syrup hardens evenly.

The Indians called the Maple, Michton.

Temperatures for maple products
when boiling at 100°C.

129.9 - Granulated Sugar
120 - Very hard Sugar
117.7 - Hard Sugar
114.4 - Soft Sugar or Taffy
113.8 - Taffy for snow
112 - Maple butter
104 - Maple syrup
100 - Boiling point of water

MAPLE BAKED APPLE

Core each apple. Fill cavity with equal amounts of butter and MAPLE SYRUP. Add a few raisins and a dash of cinnamon. Bake until tender. Serve hot.

The New England Maple Museum is in the "heart of maple country" - foothills of the Green Mts. about 8 miles North of Rutland.

The British colonists turned to maple sugar when sea trade and imported sugar was restricted due to American War for Independence.

Thos. Jefferson was Sect. of State. In 1790, he and Benjamin Rush tried to establish the maple sugar industry on a scientific basis. Only now, nearly two centuries later, is the dream coming true.

Cumberland Nuggets

Boil 1 cup maple syrup until the soft ball stage in water. Cool slightly and add 1 Tbsp. butter and beat until thickens. Add 1½ cups rice crispies. Mix well. Drop on waxed paper.

"It is an ancient chore, this maple syrup making."

"The manure piles
are smoking. The sun
is growing warmer.
Spring is just over
the hill "

BAKED MARCH COMPOTE

Core, pare and slice four apples.
Butter a baking dish, add the
apple, covering them with stale
biscuit or cake crumbs. Alternate
such layers, sprinkling apples
with brown or maple sugar and
a dash of nutmeg. After last
layer, cover with 1 cup maple
syrup.

Bake in moderate oven until
apples are barely tender. Serve
hot with whipped cream or
hard sauce - or your favourite
topping. Experiment with
variations of this recipe.

The Ojibways of the Great Lakes and the Wyandots of the Detroit River migrated in family groups to the sugar grooves where they lived in bark wigwams.

ANN ARBOR ANGEL CAKE

1½ cup Maple Syrup - ¼ cup cake flour
1¼ cup egg whites - 1 tsp. cream tartar
½ tsp. salt

Boil maple syrup until it will spin a thread. Beat egg whites until foamy, add salt and cream tartar. Beat until barely stiff. Pour hot syrup slowly to egg whites and continue to beat until mixture is cool. Fold in flour - tiny amounts at a time. Bake 1 hour at 325°.

"Winter was having

its last fling."

"The gift of the Maple trees is from a benevolent Providence."

Benjamin Rush

MAPLE MORNING CAKES

2 cups flour — 3 tsp. butter — ½ tsp. salt
2 tsp. baking powder — ⅔ cup milk
1 cup maple sugar — 1 egg — spices

Mix dough. Roll out about ½ inch thick. Spread with sugar and cinnamon or your favourite spice. To make a richer cake, spread first with butter. Roll dough and slice into 1·inch pieces. Bake 20 minutes at about 425°F.

GRANVILLE GRAPEFRUIT

CUT FRUIT IN HALF - CROSSWISE.
Remove pulp, leaving sections
intact. DRIZZLE 1½ Tbsp. of
MAPLE SYRUP OVER PREPARED
FRUIT. BROIL 3 to 4 inches
from heat for about 2 to 3 mins.
or until MAPLE SYRUP bubbles

MAPLE ON ICE CREAM

... some fifty gallons of sap to make
a gallon of good syrup, and up to
three gallons of syrup to make a
pound of sugar.

Hints from the Sugar Bush —

Maple Syrup:
- with waffles, pancakes, biscuits, French toast, cereals, fruits.
- with sweet or sour cream
- as sweetener in milk, eggnog, fruit cups
- as meat glaze
- on vegetables and fruits
- as a sauce - hot or cold
- on puddings, blancmange, custards, ice cream
- mix with nuts and butter for buns

Maple Butter:
- On breads, pancakes, cakes, French toast, etc.
- As a filling - alone or mixed
- As a topping - alone or mixed
- As a sauce

Dry Gin

	Recipe No. 1	Recipe No. 2
Dry Gin	4 parts	3 parts
Camp Maple Syrup	2 parts	2 parts
Lemon Juice	2 parts	1 part
French Vermouth		2 parts
Ice	yes	yes

Pour the ingredients in a cocktail shaker, add ice to chill, shake well and serve.

Whisky Sour

	Recipe No. 1	Recipe No. 2
Whisky	4 parts	4 parts
Orange juice		1 part
Grapefruit juice	1 part	1 part
Lemon juice	2 parts	1 part
Camp Maple Syrup	1 part	1 part
Ice	yes	yes

Recipe No. 1 using more lemon is more sour.
Recipe No. 2 is less sour but has the added orange flavour.
Pour the ingredients in a cocktail shaker, add ice to chill, shake well and serve.

York Punch

4 cups each - unsweetened grapefruit juice and orange juice
2 cups maple syrup - ¼ c. lime juice
1 tsp. each nutmeg and allspice.

Combine in 3-qt. container. Let stand about an hour, then chill. Serve over ice in punch bowl. Makes 10 cups.

CHAFING·DISH DELIGHT

1 lb. bulk pork sausage ~ 1 egg
½ cup finely crushed crackers
    (about 14 crackers)
⅓ cup milk ~ ½ tsp Sage and Basel

Combine above, mix well, beat
well (or at high speed). Shape
into about 3 dozen balls, 1¼-
inch each. (Keep hands moist
to shape the meatballs)
Brown meat, keeping the meat in
round balls~ about 10 minutes.
Pour off fat. Combine:
    ½ cup water ~ ¼ cup catsup
    3 Tbsp. Maple Sugar
    1 Tbsp. each Soy Sauce and Vinegar

Pour mixture over the meatballs. Cover and simmer about
15-20 minutes. Keep hot in
chafing dish and serve from
there.

Pennsylvania Ham

Combine and chop very fine:
1 lb. cooked ham - ½ lb. boneless beef
1 slice dry bread - ¼ c. fine parsley
Add ½ cup milk and ½ t. dry mustard
Blend well. Shape into 2" meat balls
Cook uncovered at 350°F for ½ hour.

Combine in saucepan:
¾ cup maple syrup - 2 Tbsp. cornstarch
¾ cup unsweetened pineapple
1 t. each soy sauce and lemon juice

Cook until thickened, then pour over
meat balls and cook another 20 mins.

Serve your favourite way. One
suggestion is to lightly mix
4 cups hot cooked rice with
¼ cup parsley and generous
sprinkle of dried sweet Basel.
Arrange meat balls and sauce
on top of rice and serve with
a green salad.
(There are several versions of
   this recipe).

An after dinner treat —
   IRISH CANADIAN COFFEE
(sometimes called Cafe Quebecois)
Strong freshly brewed coffee.
Add to :
   1¼ oz whiskey
   1 tsp. Maple Syrup.
earlier mixed in a wine glass.
Top with whipped cream

   Fouettée.   Un régal !

For the cocktail hour —

   Le Coureur de Bois Special

2 parts Rum — 2 parts gin
1 part jus decitron ou de limon
1 part sirop d'erable

Bien melanger à de la glace
pilée avant de servir. Délicieux!
   These recipes are from Turkey Hill, Brome,
                              Quebec

BAKED BEANS with MAPLE

Soak about 2 cups of Navy beans
overnight in about 12 cups water.
Preheat oven to 250° F. Drain
beans, put in deep crock and
cover with water. Bring to boil.
Simmer uncovered about 1 hour.
Drain and put in a well-buttered
bean crock. Add to the beans:
1 Tbsp salt, dry mustard, 1/4 lb. salt pork.
1 small diced onion, 1/3 cup brown sugar
— 3/4 cup MAPLE SYRUP —
Cover with boiling water. Cover-cook
8 hrs. at 250° F. Uncover last half hour.

Amherst Cake

½ cup sugar — ½ cup shortening
½ cup maple syrup — 1¾ cups flour
2½ tsp. baking powder — ¼ cup milk
½ cup nutmeats — 2 eggs — salt
1 tsp. vanilla or almond flavouring

Cream sugar and shortening and add maple syrup and flavouring. Beat eggs well and add. Sift together all dry ingredients, add milk and nuts and combine everything. Bake about ½ hr at 350°F.

SUGAR ON SNOW

MAPLE ICE CREAM
1 cup MAPLE SYRUP - 2 eggs
1/2 cup milk — 1 1/4 cup cream.

Boil syrup slowly for about 5 mins.
Mix yolks with milk and add the
MAPLE SYRUP to mixture, stirring
constantly. Chill.
Beat egg whites until peaked.
Add to chilled mixture, alternat-
ing with cream. Place in freezer
and allow to gel slightly. Remove
and beat with fork or whisk.
Return to freezer. Remove in
about a half hour, beat once
more, then freeze.

Another version is to use:
1 cup maple syrup — 1 pint whipping cream
2 eggs
Boil syrup and add to well beaten
eggs. Cool well and add whipped
cream. Stir from time to time.
Freeze.

124

MAPLE MEN

1 cup butter — 2 tbsp. maple syrup
1½ cups maple sugar (or dark brown)
1 egg — 4 tsp. grated orange peel
3 cups sifted flour — ½ tsp. salt
2 tsps. each baking soda and cinnamon
½ tsp. ground cloves — 1 tsp. ginger

Cream butter and sugar and add
egg. Beat lightly. Add maple
syrup and orange peel. Mix well.
Sift together remaining ingredients
and add to creamed mixture.
Chill the dough. Roll out on
lightly floured surface to about
¼ inch or slightly less. Cut
with gingerbread (MAPLE!) man
cutter. Space about 1-inch apart
on cookie sheet (do not grease).
Bake about 9 minutes at 375°F.
Cool a few seconds and remove
to a rack.
MAPLE MEN can be dressed up
with raisins and icing.

"What can a man do better on the face of the earth than to cultivate and beautify it? While ever ready to depart, the lover of beautiful trees should act as if he expected to live a thousand years." Plant a Sugar Maple today! The New England Farmer 1832

Maple Mincemeat

1½ qts. chopped meat — 1½ lbs. raisins
4½ qts. chopped apples — 4 tsp. nutmeg
(Keep 1 qt. water in which meat was cooked). 1½ qts. MAPLE SYRUP
8 tsp. Cloves — 10 tsp. Cinnamon
2 tsp. each salt and pepper

Cook over low heat until the apples are soft and mixture is thick. Can or freeze until ready to use.

This is an old-fashioned recipe with similar versions across Canada and U.S.A.

BRAN MUFFINS
(Cumberland Co., N.S. recipe)

¾ cup maple syrup — 2 eggs
Add 2½ cups crushed bran flakes
Let stand 5 minutes.
Using wooden spoon, beat in
1 cup sour milk (keep lumpy)
Stir in :
1 cup all-purpose flour
1 tsp. baking soda - ½ cup nutmeats

Bake about 20 mins. at 400°.

MAPLE SQUASH

3 lb. baked squash — 3 Tbsp. butter
⅓ cup maple syrup — ½ tsp. salt

Scoop out pulp. Add butter, salt
and syrup. Beat well. Bake
in greased casserole, at
350° for 40-45 minutes.

New Brunswick Chicken

6 boned chicken breasts
Cooking oil — 2 eggs, beaten

Dip chicken in beaten eggs and
saute until golden brown, adding
1 Tbsp. lemon juice to the oil.
Put chicken in a serving/oven dish.
Cover with mixture of ½ c. maple sugar,
1 cup light cream, 1 cup milk. Bake
at 350° until meat is tender.
Serve with long-grained rice, apricots
and any assortment of such fruits.

The Indians called white sugar, "French snow"; early explorers referred to the sap of the Maple as "Maple Manna."

CANADIAN DELIGHT

4-5 medium sweet potatoes
    (boiled in skins)
4-5 medium apples — ¼ cup butter
1 cup MAPLE SYRUP — salt
Buttered crumbs

Add pared, sliced apples to syrup. Add butter and pinch of salt. Cook slowly until apples are tender. Pare boiled sweet potatoes and slice half into well-buttered pan. Spoon half of syrup mixture over potatoes. Repeat. Top generously with buttered crumbs. Bake at 400° until reheated and crumbs browned. This is some good!

NELSON CUPCAKES

Measure 1¾ cup all-purpose flour.
Sift with 2½ tsp. baking powder
     and ½ tsp. salt
Flour ½ cup broken walnuts
Cream ¼ cup shortening. Gradually
add ¼ cup white SUGAR and
     1 cup grated maple sugar.
Beat 2 eggs until slightly thickened.
Add dry ingredients alternately with
½ cup cream. Add nuts. Fill cup
cake papers ¾ full. Bake at
375°F about 15-20 minutes. Cover
with butter frosting which has been
maple flavoured. Garnish with
walnut halves or crushed walnuts.

"We used to make our sap spiles
even though "store-boughten' ones
only cost a nickel ... We never
bought anything we could make."

Monty Washburn
The Salt Box
Kittery Pt., Maine

Clarence Alphonse Gagnon 1881-1942
Illustration for Maria Chapdelaine
egg tempra/paper
21.9 × 22.0 cm.
The McMichael Canadian Collection
Gift of Col. R.S. McLaughlin
1969.4.51

Maple Baked Onions

8 medium onions ~ 1 Tbsp soft butter
3 tbsp. each Maple Syrup and Tomato J.
Salt and Pepper to taste.

Skin onions, cut crosswise,
place in greased baking dish.
Combine ingredients and pour
over onions. Cover and bake
about 1 hour or until tender –
at about 350°.

VERMONT   SUGAR

IN THE EARLY SPRING

When we see our first robin in the Green Mountain
State, when the cold February blasts and snows give
way to the first March thaw, Vermont sugar makers
climb up their maple mountains to drill the new "tap
holes" into the hard rock maples. They select only the
mature maples in the "sugar bush" to produce the sweet
maple sap. *Before a tree is mature enough to be tapped
it must be some 40 years old, "a foot through" and some
60 ft. tall.* With the buckets hung on the sap spouts
they wait for the coming of warm days with freezing
cold nights to make the sap run. Actually, sap doesn't
run, it merely drips and a "good run" means that the
sap drips faster.

In one of his lectures, Robert Frost said that his State was "milk and sugar country." Then he smiled and added, "We get what runs from Trees and what runs from cows."

COTTAGE CHEESE PIE

1 cup cottage cheese — 1 cup milk
3/4 cup maple syrup — 1/2 tsp. cinnamon
1/8 tsp. salt — 2 (well beaten) eggs

Blend everything. Put into unbaked 9" pastry shell. Bake at 350° until crust is browned and done.

This is a Shilbe recipe from the Ontario cookbook, TEMPTING TREATS.

"When a farmer sees 'coon tracks in a snowbank, he begins looking at his sap pails. Spring isn't far off."

MAPLE GINGER BISCUITS

12 oz flour — 3 Tbsp. maple sugar
4 oz sugar — 4 ozs. butter
1 Tbsp. gr. ginger — ½ tsp. bicar-
bonate of soda

Melt butter in syrup, beat in
flour, mix well. Roll out on
floured board, cut into rounds.
Bake 10-15 mins.

GRADES FOR MAPLE SYRUP:

No. 1. - Uniform in color, no clouding, "Extra light", "Light" or
"Medium". Characteristic
maple flavour increasing with
depth of colour. No odor or
other taste.

No. 2. - Uniform color, no clouding.
"Amber", stronger maple flavour.
No fermentation or odor.

No. 3. - Characteristic maple
flavour - no fermentation.

Maple sugar was the "long sweetenin'" for culinary uses. "Small beer" was made with maple sap and yeast— "a very pleasant drink, suffic- iently spirituous." Before the Revolution the market was glutted. England's laws dis- allowed importation of maple sugar from America.

History of Agric. in N.Y. State
Hendrick, 1933

MAPLE GLAZED CARROTS

8 carrots, peeled — 1 Tbsp. vinegar
3/4 cup boiling water — 3/4 tsp. salt
3 Tbsp. melted butter — 1/4 tsp. salt
3 Tbsp. maple syrup
Cut carrots into sticks. Add water and salt and boil -about 15 mins. Drain and layer in baking pan. Combine ingredients and drizzle over carrots, Bake 30 mins. at 350°F. Turn to glaze both sides.

In response to my inquiry, the Philatelic Promotion section of Canada Post wrote, " Canada Post has never issued a stamp to honour the Maple Industry." Why not lobby for such a stamp—a salute to Canada's first industry.

BROWN BREAD with MAPLE

2 cups corn meal — 1 cup rye flour
1 cup white flour — 1 cup sour milk
1½ tsp. soda — 1 cup maple syrup
1 cup milk — large dark raisins

Dissolve soda in sour milk. Mix corn meal and flour and salt. Add all the milk. Mix well and add the maple syrup and raisins. Pour into well buttered baking mold and cover. Steam about 2 hours.
Serve hot with baked beans or use as a sweet bread, cold and sliced thin, and lightly buttered.

QUEBEC CAKES

2 tsp. soda
1 pint each sour cream and sour milk
Flour — enough to make a soft dough
3/4 tsp. cream of tartar
3 eggs (beaten) — 1 tsp. salt

Beat the eggs and blend with the sour milk and cream. Stir the flour, soda, cream of tartar and salt. Roll out the dough on lightly floured board. When about 3/4" thick, cut in strips of desired length or in circles, and fry in hot deep fat.

Serve with nearly hot maple syrup.

In Quebec there are maple syrup experts, similar to the connoisseurs of wine. In each instance the expert can identify the quality as well as the region where it was produced.

LAC ST. JEAN PUDDING

1 cup cooked rice — 1 cup maple syrup
3 beaten eggs — ½ cup raisins
2 cups milk — dash of Nutmeg

Combine gently. Set baking dish
in pan of hot water and bake
about 1 hour at 325°F.

"The people here treat one with
maple sap; it is now the season
when the sap flows from the trees.
It is delicious, admirably refreshing, and very pure ... One thing is
certain... the Indians before the
colonists arrived here, did not
know how to make sugar. They
were satisfied after they had
boiled the sap two or three
times, to thicken it into a
syrup, which was tasty enough."

Journal d'un Voyage, Vol. v
Charlevoix, 1744

Maple Meringue

Beat 1 egg white and add 1 cup confectioners' sugar and ¼ cup maple sugar. Beat until lightly peaked. Sprinkle with maple sugar. Nutmeats chopped very fine can be added — try tossing them lightly in dab of maple syrup!

MAPLE SHORTBREADS

1 cup butter — 1/4 cup maple sugar
2 cups all-purpose flour — dash salt
1 1/2 cups coconut — 1/4 cup currants
1/3 cup chopped almonds —
1 can evaporated milk

Cream butter (margarine or shortening)
with grated maple sugar. Blend
in flour and pat the dough into
a greased pan - about 9-inch square.
Bake about 20 mins. at 350°F.
Combine rest of ingredients and
spread over the shortbread.
Bake another 15 mins. (golden brown)
Cool well. Cut into small squares.
Sprinkle with grated maple
sugar.

Wise men set hard maples along the
boundary lines of their farms...a
source of revenue, for these low-
branched, isolated trees give an
abundant flow of sap in the
early spring. The Tree Book, 1935

New Brunswick has always been a "sweet" Province. Frances Beaven wrote about her life in the bush in 1845. She loved the "sugar-maker's bark-covered hut." With her "shanty loaf" of bread, tea made from hemlock or winter-green and her "sweetening being handy bye," she had all the sus-tenance needed. David Folster

SWEET POTATO PUDDING

3 cups sweet potatoes - raw, grated
½ cup maple syrup - ½ cup sugar
1 cup milk - 2 Tbsp. soft butter
1 tsp. nutmeg - 2 eggs, well beaten
½ tsp. each chopped nuts, salt

Beat eggs and add to a mixture of all other ingredients. Butter a shallow baking dish and cook at 375°F for about an hour.

MAPLE WALNUT FILLING

¼ cup sesame seeds
½ cup chopped walnuts
3 Tablespoons Maple Syrup

Combine in a small bowl.
Blend thoroughly.

During and after the American Revolution there were many idealists who believed that Maple Sugar could compete with cane sugar on the market. Serious attempts were made to build up a great maple sugar industry in New York. The problem was that business methods proposed were too advanced for the primitive equipment and conditions. So-sugar-making remained a home industry for a long time.

MAPLE FILLING

Combine:
½ cup soft butter — 1 cup brown sugar
⅔ cup white sugar — 4 Tbsp. flour
1 tsp. cinnamon — 1 Tbsp. Maple Syrup
Sprinkle on top: ½ cup chopped nuts

DOYLE GRANOLA
Mix together well:
¼ c. large uncooked rolled oats
2 c. wheat germ — 1 c. sunflower seeds
2 c. unsweetened shredded coconut
1 c. dark brown sugar — 1 c. sesame seeds
Add to above:
¾ c. Maple Syrup — 1 c. corn oil
¼ t. salt — 1 t. Vanilla

Spread thinly in pans. Bake at 275°-
300° for about 20 mins. or until
toasted. Watch carefully not to burn.

"By the help of my trees and my
bees, we yearly procure the
sweetenin' we want."

Different regions in Canada and U.S.A. make different versions of Maple Sugar Pie.

MAPLE SUGAR PIE[1]

Enough maple sugar to cover bottom of an unbaked shell. Dot with butter and sprinkle with nutmeg. Pour about ⅔ cup cream over pie filling. Make fancy pattern with strips of pastry. Bake at 375°F until sugar is melted.

MAPLE SUGAR PIE[2]

1 cup maple sugar — 1 cup sweet cream
½ cup butter — 1 egg, beaten lightly
Combine butter and sugar. Add egg and then the cream. Fill unbaked pastry shell and cook like a custard.

Charles Darwin thought that the flow of the sap was "that most nebulous of subjects."

MAPLE SUGAR PIE[3]

2 cups milk — ⅔ cup maple sugar
1 egg yolk — 2 Tbsp. corn starch

Cook about 5 minutes in double
boiler. Cool and add dash of
Vanilla. Turn into shell already
baked, frost and brown. (Frost
means meringue made with egg
white beaten stiff, adding
1 Tbsp. sugar and 10 drops Vanilla.

MAPLE SUGAR PIE[4]

1 cup MAPLE SUGAR — ½ cup cream
1 egg - butter, size of a walnut
1 Tbsp. flour — dash of pepper

Cream sugar and butter. Beat egg
and combine with flour, pepper
and cream and add to sugar and
butter. Pour into unbaked shell.
Cover with a crust. Bake at 450°F
about 10 mins, then reduce to
325°F.
(This is an old Vermont recipe)

un petit déjeuner délicieux et très
nourrissant.

GRANOLA

Combine dry ingredients —
7 cups rolled oats — 1 cup wheat germ
½ cup sesame seeds — ¼ cup Filberts
½ cup sunflower seeds — ½ cup raisins
1 cup MAPLE SUGAR (or brown sugar)
½ tsp. salt
Combine wet ingredients —
½ cup MAPLE SYRUP — ½ cup oil
½ cup boiling water — ½ tsp. Vanilla
Mix _all_ ingredients well. Bake
in 325° oven about 1 hour —or
until golden brown. Stir now and then.
Cool and store. Keeps well.
Serve with milk.

There is an old saying in Sugar Country,
"if you don't like the weather, wait
a minute". So, when the South wind
blows or the night is warm or a
"cold snap" freezes everything,
The Sugar Maker goes back to
the woodpile until the sap runs.

146

MAPLE KRINGLES

1/4 cup maple syrup — 1 egg
1 cup semisweet chocolate pieces
2 Tbsp. butter — 1/2 cup coconut
1/2 cup dry roasted peanuts or
   your favourite nutmeats
1/2 tsp. vanilla — dash of salt

Melt chocolate in butter over low
heat. Remove and cool to lukewarm. Add egg, beating until
glossy. Add syrup, salt and
vanilla, and mix well. Add to
chocolate/butter mixture. Stir
in flaked coconut and nuts.
Chill slightly.

Form a long roll, about 10 inches.
Wrap and chill. Slice about
1/4 inch thick, making between
30 and 40 MAPLE KRINGLES

"An ideal Sugar Bush should have a
foliage cover so complete that no
direct sunlight penetrates to the
forest floor."

Comme dessert ou avec le goûter

BRANDY SNAPS

½ cup MAPLE SYRUP — ½ cup butter
(½ cup molasses) — 1 cup flour
⅔ cup granulated sugar
1 tsp. ground ginger
2 tsp. Brandy

Bring SYRUP and molasses to a boil.
Remove from heat, add butter.
Sift dry ingredients and slowly
combine with syrup mixture. Add
Brandy and stir. Drop by
teaspoonful on greased baking
sheet. Bake at 300° about 10
minutes - should look "lacy".

Loosen each cookie and gently
roll around the handle of a
wooden spoon. Slide off and
cool on rack. Serve filled
                a Turkey Hill recipe
                Brome, Quebec

FLUFFY MAPLE SAUCE

Separate two eggs. Beat whites
until glossy, add dash of salt and
1/4 cup white sugar. Beat more.
Beat yolks until lemon coloured.
Add 1/4 cup white sugar. Beat more.
Combine the two mixtures, fold in
1 tsp. pure maple or maple extract.
(Some people prefer a stronger
maple flavour). Chill until ready
to use.

Vanilla Pie

Make favourite pie shell.

Blend following ingredients and cook until starts to thicken. Cool.

1 cup maple syrup — ½ cup white sugar
1 egg (beaten)   — 2 Tbsp. flour
1 cup water   — 1 tsp. vanilla

Combine the following into a crumbly texture.

1 cup brown sugar — 1 cup flour
¼ cup shortening — ½ tsp. soda
½ tsp. baking powder

Pour first mixture into shell and top with second mixture.

Bake for about 45 minutes at 350°F.

The Mennonite ladies of Waterloo Co, (Ontario) baked dozens of this pie for the Elmira Maple Syrup Festival. (See Introduction)

MAPLE LEBKUCHEN

1 cup maple syrup — ¾ cup br. sugar
1 Tbsp. lemon juice — 1 egg
1 tsp. grated orange rind — ½ tsp. soda
2¾ cups flour — ⅓ chopped ginger
1 tsp. each cloves, allspice, nutmeg,
                                    cinnamon
⅛ cup slivered almonds

Bring maple syrup to a boil. Add
sugar, egg, juice and rind. Sift
dry ingredients together and
blend with other mixture. Add
candied ginger and almonds.
Chill overnight.

Roll wee bit of dough at a time,
about ¼" thick. Use favourite
cutter - bake 1" apart on greased
sheet. Bake 10-12 minutes.
Remove quickly - cool - store in
airtight container that contains a
slice of apple. You might want
to lightly glaze warm COOKIES!

MAPLE TOFFEE

1 cup butter ⌐ ½ cup sugar
¾ cup maple syrup ⌐ 3 Tbsp. water
1 cup chopped blanched almonds
1 cup finely chopped blanched almonds
4 4½ oz. milk chocolate candy bars
                                    (melted)

Melt butter, add sugar, water,
and maple syrup in a large
saucepan. Cook to hard ball
stage - stirring constantly.
Quickly add the coarsely chopped
toasted almonds. Spread in
a large shallow buttered
baking pan. Cool.

Turn out on wax paper.
Cover with half the chocolate,
sprinkle with half the finely
chopped almonds (toasted).
Spread again with chocolate
and then with nuts. Chill
thoroughly. Serve in broken
pieces.

GROTON PUDDING

2 Tbsp. MAPLE SYRUP — 3 ozs butter
½ cup brown sugar — dash nutmeg
4 slices stale French bread cut
into small cubes.

Put syrup and butter and sugar
in pan. Stir until it boils-about
3 minutes. Add the bread and
serve when it is well saturated
in the maple mixture.

Pumpkin Mousse with Maple

2½ cups heavy cream — Pecan halves
1 29oz can pumpkin pie filling
2 envelopes plus 1 tsp. unflavoured gelatin
2 tsp. maple syrup
½ tsp. granulated sugar.

Using a large bowl, whip 2 cups of
the cream until soft peak stage.
(do not beat stiff). Stir gelatine
into ½ cup of pumpkin. Stir over
moderate heat until mixture is
smooth and almost simmering.
Remove from heat.
Put remaining pumpkin in a large
bowl and stir rapidly as you add
the hot gelatine mixture. Stir
in maple syrup and about ½ cup
of whipped cream.
Cover with plastic and chill at
least 4 hours or overnight. Before
serving, whip remaining ½ cup
cream and the sugar until stiff.
Spoon on top of Mousse. Garnish
with pecans. (Fills an 8-10 cup mold)

SUGARIE MOUSSE

7 eggs (separated) — 1 cup MAPLE SUGAR
2 envelopes gelatin (dissolve in ¾ cup coffee)
2 tsp. cornstarch — ½ cup whipping cream
1½ cups boiling milk — 1 Tbsp. sugar
slivered almonds or nutmeg sugar to top.

Add sugar and cornstarch to beaten
egg yolks. Beat about 3 minutes
and gradually add the milk. Stir
over low heat — wooden spoon is
recommended. <u>Do not boil</u>.
When custard thickens, add gelatin
and beat well.

Beat egg whites with salt and 1 Tbsp.
sugar. When soft peaks form fold
whites into custard. Cool slightly.

Whip cream and gently add to
cooled custard. Makes an 8-cup
mold. Chill overnight or at least
5 hours. Decorate with almonds,
nutmeg sugar or sprinkle with fine
maple sugar.

BENNINGTON SALAD

Pare carefully, core and quarter
six apples. Carefully skewer
them together and fill each
cavity with a mixture of
1 Tbsp. butter and 6 Tbsp. maple
sugar, with a wee bit of nutmeg
on top. (This should be ample
for six apples)

Place in baking pan, adding 1cup
of water. Bake until barely tender.
Cool and chill. Just before
serving, remove skewers, put
4 quarters on crisp greens,
sprinkle with slivered almonds
and top with your favourite
dressing.

Maple Bran Muffins

¾ cup natural wheat bran — 1 egg
½ cup each - Maple syrup and milk
¼ cup vegetable oil — 3 tsp. baking pwdr.
1¼ cups whole wheat flour
⅓ cup chopped walnuts — ½ tsp. salt

Combine MAPLE SYRUP, bran and milk.
Add egg and oil. Combine remaining
ingredients and mix with first
until moistened. Spoon into
greased muffin tins. Bake at
200°C (400°F) for 20 minutes.
Makes 1 dozen muffins.
                    (Quebec recipe)

"The dear dear muffins of home"
          Wm. M. Thackeray

Wood Engraving by Lucille Oille
from <u>The Owl Pen</u> by Kenneth MacN. Wells

Maple Syrup Tarts

1 cup Maple syrup - 6 Tbsp. flour
½ cup water - 3 egg yolks, beaten
1 Tbsp. butter - ¼ cup nuts, chopped
12 baked tart shells

Heat maple syrup in double boiler.
Mix flour and water until smooth.
Stir gradually into heated syrup and
cook until thickened (10 minutes).
Stir constantly. Mix some of the
hot mixture with the yolks, stir
into remainder in double boiler and
continue cooking 3 to 4 minutes.
Remove from heat, stir in butter
and walnuts. Cool slightly and
pour into pie shell or tart shells.
Top with whipped cream or
Meringue.

Meringue: Beat 2 egg whites and
dash of salt until soft peaks. Add sugar
(¼ c.) gradually and beat until stiff.
Spread over filling. Bake 15 mins.
350° or 5 mins. at 425° F.

MAPLE CHOCOLATE SYRUP

1 cup MAPLE SYRUP — 1/4 cup cocoa
1/4 cup water — 1 tsp. Vanilla - salt

Combine and boil a few minutes.
(Sometimes I bring to boil before
adding Vanilla and salt.)
Store in refrigerator. Use on
ice cream or for hot or cold
chocolate milk.

ANNAPOLIS VALLEY PUDDING

3 apples — 1 cup Maple syrup
1/2 cup apple juice — 1 cup flour
1 egg — 1/4 cup butter - 1/2 cup milk
1/4 cup brown sugar - 1/2 tsp. salt
2 tsp. baking powder

Peel, core and slice apples. Add
syrup and juice. Simmer in covered
saucepan 5 mins. Put in buttered
baking dish.

(continued next page)

Continued –
ANNAPOLIS VALLEY PUDDING

Cream butter and brown sugar.
Add egg and mix well. Combine
flour, baking powder, salt.
Add dry ingredients and milk
to creamed mixture. Mix well.
Spread batter evenly over apple-
syrup mixture. Bake at 180°C.
(350°F) for 35-40 mins. Serve warm
with ice cream or whipped cream.
About 6 servings.

Jean-Baptiste Cyr, an Acadian,
came to New Brunswick in 1770. He
had a fine stand of maples near
Sugar Island outside of Fredericton.
His customary inquiry to travellers
was, "Voulez-vous de quoi a croquer"
Soon he was called "Le Vieux
Croc" and in time the area was
called Crocks Point. Later he
moved to Madawaska, a region
famous for maple products.
                    David Polster

162

MAPLE FROSTED ORANGE SLICES

1 cup maple syrup - well heated
Add twelve seedless-orange slices.
They should lie flat. Bring to
boil, then remove from heat and
cool. Spoon syrup over slices.
Repeat boiling/cooling about
six times or until syrup has
been absorbed. Put slices on a
wire rack and stand overnight.

Combine about ½ cup confectioners
sugar with ¼ cup water - heat
but do not boil. Cut each
orange slice in half and dip
in the sugar syrup. Drain, cool
and dry on rack.

Store in covered tin. Should
keep at least a month.

"If the sap could be evaporated
without heat the sugar would
be white as snow."

Simcoe Sweet Bread

1 cup Maple Syrup — 1 egg, well eaten
2 Tbsp. melted shortening
Grated rind of one orange

Blend above ingredients. Sift dry
ingredients:
3 tsp. baking powder — 2½ cups flour
½ tsp. each soda and salt
¾ cup slivered almonds or
            finely chopped walnuts
Combine the two mixtures and
add ¾ cup orange juice.

Bake at 350° for 60 minutes, using a
well-greased loaf pan.

"Good God, how sweet are all
things here."
    attributed to Charles Cotton
    by Isaak Walton

"PASTRY
IMPRESSIONS"

PRALINES

2 cups MAPLE SYRUP
1/2 cups broken pecans or walnuts

Cook syrup until it makes a
soft ball in cold water. Let it
stand until boiling stops- about
1 minute. Pour into lightly
buttered pie pan. Sprinkle nuts
on top. Serve cold by spoonfuls.

"The first makers of Maple sugar
used wooden troughs (auges de bois)
which were placed at foot of each
tree_ to collect sap." The spiles
(goudrelles) leading the sap from
the tree to the trough were a
tongue of cedar (platine de
cedre) about 6" long.
                    Edmond Savoie
                    Beauce County

MAPLE HAM

½ cup each maple syrup and crumbs
1 egg beaten — ⅛ tsp. ground cloves
1 lb. ground cooked ham — parsley
12 canned peach halves, drained

Combine egg, crumbs, syrup, cloves,
and ham. Shape into 12 balls.
Place peaches, hollow sides up,
in greased shallow baking pan.
Nest a ham ball in each peach.
Bake at 350°, about 25 minutes.
Garnish with parsley — or celery
tops.

" that divinest of all moments in the
year, when in man and brute and
leafless tree, the sap once more stirs."

MAPLE SUNDAE SAUCE

½ cup Maple Syrup — ½ cup nutmeats
— 8 marshmallows —

Combine Syrup and Marshmallows.
Cook over hot water until smooth.
Cool. Add chopped nutmeats just
before serving.

ITHACA SWEETS

½ cup maple syrup — ½ tsp. vanilla
½ cup water — 1 cup sugar
1 stiffly beaten egg white
¼ cup slivered almonds

Combine and bring to a boil the
syrup, sugar, and water. When
at the hard-ball stage, add
flavouring and pour over the
peaked egg whites. Add almonds.
Beat again. When stiff enough,
drop on to wax paper to
harden.

"Prepare for making maple sugar,
which is more pleasant and patriotic
than that ground by the hand of
slavery, and boiled down by the
heat of misery."

The Old Farmers Almanack
1803

167

"Sap runs before a rain and after a snow."

a sap slogan

MAPLE - COFFEE COOKIES

1 cup maple syrup — ¾ cup sugar
  (maple sugar or brown sugar)
2 tsp. ginger — 1 tsp. salt
1 cup butter (shortening can be used)
1½ tsp. soda in ¼ cup cold water
4 cups sifted flour — 2 eggs

Stir ginger, sugar and salt in a saucepan. Add maple syrup and butter and bring to boil for 1 min. Cool. Add soda in water, beaten eggs and 3 cups flour. Keep dough soft. Roll out ½ inch thick. Cut into circles. Bake 15 mins. at 350°. Eat with breakfast coffee.

MAPLE WHEAT PUDDING

2 shredded-wheat biscuits
2 cups hot milk — 2 eggs
1/3 cup each molasses + maple syrup
1 tsp. cinnamon — 1 Tbsp. butter
Pinch of salt   (or margarine)

Crumble shredded-wheat into a bowl and cover with the milk. Combine eggs, slightly beaten, salt, molasses, maple syrup and cinnamon; add to first mixture, mixing well. Pour into buttered casserole and dot with the butter. Bake at 350° about 50 minutes. Sweet and spicy, this needs only cream, plain or whipped, or a commercial topping. Serves 4-6.

from Maple Cooking, © 1969, B. Vaughan
Stephen Greene Press
Brattleboro, Vermont

"He offered us each a little syrup. Each of us took a sip. It was some good."

MAPLE CUSTARD PIE

½ cup grated maple sugar — ¼ cup white sugar
1½ cups milk — 2 egg yolks
½ cup milk — ⅛ tsp. salt - 2 egg whites
1 tsp. maple extract.

Combine sugars, egg yolks, milk and salt and beat well. Cook until mixture thickens —about 5 minutes. Add maple extract.

Beat egg whites until peaked. Gently fold into custard. Pour into graham cracker or unbaked 9-inch shell. Bake 30-40 minutes at about 300°.

N.Y. State Indians celebrated the return of spring with a "maple moon" festival and a special maple dance.

New York Bran Muffins

Combine:
    1 cup sour cream
    1 cup maple syrup
    2 eggs, slightly beaten
Sift together:
    1 cup flour and 1 tsp. baking soda
Stir in:
    1 cup bran flakes
    1/3 cup raisins
    1/3 cup chopped nuts

Combine and spoon into greased muffin tins. Bake 20 mins. at 400° F.

The Sugar Maple is the offical tree of New York State.

Maple sap contains on average 97.5 % water, 2.4 % sugar and 0.1 % mineral matter.

MAPLE-MOLASSES TAFFY

1½ cups sugar — 1 cup light molasses
½ cup maple syrup — ¼ cup water
2 Tbsp. butter — ½ cup nutmeats
¼ tsp. baking soda

Combine sugar, maple syrup and molasses with the water in a large saucepan. Cook gently for about 20 minutes, stirring all the time. Increase heat, keep stirring and cook until hard ball stage (in cold water) – probably about 45 minutes. Add soda, butter and chopped nuts. Pour into a well-greased pan. After about 15 minutes, pull the mixture until light golden and nearly opaque. Make ropes and cut with scissors. Wrap individually in wax paper. Makes about 6 dozen 1-inch pieces.

Despite some prodigious yields, the
average mature maple produces about
12 gallons of sap, or 3 pounds sugar per
season.   Dept. of Agriculture

MAPLE GINGERBREAD

1 cup sour cream (thick) — 1 egg
1 cup maple syrup — ½ cup sugar
½ tsp. each ginger and salt
1 tsp. cinnamon — 2 cups sifted flour
2 tsp. baking soda

Combine sugar, spices and salt.
Add sour cream and gently stir
in maple syrup to which soda
has been added. Mix well and
add flour and then the egg, well
beaten. Butter a pan - bake in
slow oven - 325°F - about 45 mins.
Serve plain or with maple
flavoured whipped cream.

1981 was a GOOD year for Maple
Syrup. Highest since 1926 for N.H.

173

MAPLE NUT BUTTER FROSTING

Blend ⅓ cup butter with 3 cups confectioners sugar. Stir in ⅓ cup MAPLE SYRUP, and ¼ cup finely chopped nuts. Beat well for easy spreading.

CANDIED SWEET POTATOES

Cook, peel and slice sweet potatoes. Drizzle maple syrup generously over potatoes and dot with butter. Cook uncovered in the oven until potatoes are glazed. (Final glaze can be done on top burner). Baste often.

BROME QUICK BREAD

2 cups all-purpose flour
3 cups whole-wheat flour
2 tsp. double-acting baking powder
2 tsp. baking soda – 1½ tsp. salt
2½ cups buttermilk – 1¼ cup maple syrup
⅓ cup vegetable oil

Grease two loaf pans. Preheat oven to 350°F. Combine first six ingredients. In another bowl combine buttermilk, syrup and oil. Stir gently into first mixture. Spoon into pans.

Bake about 50 minutes. Cool briefly, then remove loaves to rack.

A great quantity of sap can be taken from a Sugar maple in one season; however, a record quantity may "kill the golden goose" and also terminate the life of the Tree.

PINEAPPLE-DATE SALAD

8oz. pkg. cream cheese
1 cup MAPLE SYRUP
1 cup CRUSHED PINEAPPLE (DRAINED)
1 cup chopped dates
1 cup chopped nuts
1 large container of Cool Whip

Mix softened cream cheese and
MAPLE SYRUP until smooth. Add
remaining ingredients. Put into
ring mold. Freeze and remove
from freezer just before serving.

Prairie du Sac, Wisconsin

"There is a sumptuous variety
about the New England weather
that compels the stranger's
admiration — and regret. The
weather is always doing some-
thing there...(more so) in spring.
In the spring I have counted
136 different kinds of weather,
inside of four and twenty hours."
                    Mark Twain, 1876

176

Exchanging Ideas

SWEET SYRUP SYLLABUB

2 cups milk — ¾ cup maple sugar
(substitute here — 1¼ c. milk & 1 c. maple
4 egg yolks — 1 tsp. almond   syrup)
1 Tbsp. flour — 1 pint whipped cream

Bring milk barely to a boil and add
flour and maple syrup (or sugar!)
Cook about 10 mins. in double boiler.

Add beaten egg yolks to above
mixture, stirring slowly. Cook
about 5 mins. while stirring.
Add almond and immediately remove
from heat. Cool. Serve this
syllabub with whipped cream
sprinkled with nutmeg.

171

"I've eaten so much country maple sugar recently... that I shall presently be indistinguishable from a French-Canadian."

Henry Beston

POLISH SAUERKRAUT

2 lbs. fresh SAUERKRAUT
1 small fresh cabbage - shredded fine
2 small onions - cut very fine
1 cup maple syrup

Cook the Sauerkraut and cabbage until fresh vegetable is tender. At the same time, sauté the onions but do not brown, and add to the cooking sauerkraut mixture. Add the maple syrup - mix well and continue to cook slowly.

Baked sliced Polish sausage can be added or served on the top of the Sauerkraut, garnished with hot maple syrup.

BEAUCE HAM and FRUIT

2 eggs, slightly beaten ⁓ dash salt
3/4 cup crushed saltines
1/2 cup maple syrup
1/8 tsp. ground cloves
1 lb. ground cooked ham
6 canned peach halves, drained
6 canned pear halves, drained
Nutmeg - Parsley - orange rind

Make 12 balls, combining the ground ham, eggs, crackers, syrup and cloves. Place into fruit halves and place in greased baking dish. Each fruit half, hollow side up, will hold a ball of ham mixture. Bake about a half hour at 350°. Sprinkle very lightly with nutmeg and orange rind and garnish with sprigs of parsley.

"All historic nobility rests
on the possession and
use of the land."
Ralph Waldo Emerson

179

In the early days the settlers made only enough syrup for their families. Most of the sap was made into hard sugar and kept in open air for a year.

MAPLE SUGAR SOUFFLÉ

1 lb. maple sugar — ½ lb. brown sugar
2 egg whites — 1 cup nutmeats
½ cup each chopped figs, raisins
½ cup each grated lemon peel, water

Boil sugar and water until tough threads form. Beat whites to a foam & gradually add the hot syrup. When slightly hardened, add other ingredients.

"The most delightful of all farm work, or of all rural occupations is at hand, namely, sugar-making..."
John Burroughs
Winter Sunshine, 1881

MAPLE DUMPLINGS

2 cups flour — 4 tsp. baking powder
1/4 cup shortening — 2/3 cup milk
2 cups maple syrup — 1 tsp. salt

Mix dry ingredients. Cut in shortening. Make depression in mixture. Add milk and stir until mixture is moist. Turn out on floured board. Knead gently — fold and press several times. Roll to fit a pan 8" x 8" or a 6" x 10". Cut into 8 rectangles and brush with milk. Heat syrup to boiling and pour into baking pan. Arrange dough on top. Bake uncovered at 425°F until surface golden brown — 15 - 20 minutes. Baste once with hot syrup.

"The March winds had blown themselves out. Rainy April had set in ... Maple sap was flowing freely, and the woods and maple orchards were filled with sounds of industry." Henry Ward Beecher
1868

"The Indian sugar... owes its peculiar taste to the birch-bark vessels that the sap is gathered in."
Catharine Parr Traill

Indian Sugaring Camp

YANKEE CAKE

1 cup maple syrup — ⅔ cup shortening
⅓ cup sugar — 2¼ cups flour
3 tsp. baking powder — 1 tsp. salt
¼ cup milk — 3 egg whites, beaten

Grease layer cake pans. Preheat oven to 350°F. Cream sugar and shortening. Add syrup and stir well. Sift flour salt, baking powder, add along with milk to the mixture. Fold in egg whites. Bake at 45 mins. Cool on racks.

PETERBOROUGH PUMPKIN PIE

7/8 cup milk — 1½ cups pumpkin
2 beaten eggs — ¾ cup Maple Syrup
½ tsp. each ginger and nutmeg
¼ tsp. cloves — 1 tsp. cinnamon
— dash of salt —

Combine and pour into unbaked
pastry shell. Bake 10 mins. at
450°, then reduce to 350° for
40 mins. Remove and sprinkle
top with:
1 tsp. melted butter — ¼ cup nuts
2 tsp. maple sugar
Return to oven for 5 minutes.

"For the sugar cakes, a board of
basswood is prepared, about
five or six inches wide, with
molds gouged in the form of
bears, diamonds, crosses,
rabbits, turtles, etc. When
the sugar is cooked it is
poured into the molds."
                    Elizabeth Therese Baird

To boil sap under the open sky, we used three kettles hanging from poles resting on forked posts. A "hell fire" (feu d'enfer) was kept night and day. The rain made the work a trying affair

Edmond Savoie

MAPLE BREAD PUDDING

1 cup maple syrup — 8 slices bread
3 tbsp. butter — 3 eggs, beaten
1½ cups milk — dash of salt

Boil syrup 5 minutes. Butter one side each slice of bread. Dip each slice in syrup and put 2 slices, buttered side up – in bottom of buttered loaf pan. Arrange rest of bread in layers. Combine eggs, rest of syrup, salt and milk. Pour over bread. Bake at 325°F. until custard is set and top is golden brown — above 50 mins.   6 - 8 servings.

(1 cup maple sugar can be used in place of syrup.)

CREAMY CANDY

Stir together ¼ cup creamy peanut butter and ½ cup maple syrup. When mixture is smooth, add 1½ cups thick cream. Pour the mixture into a freezing tray.

"Remember the days of old, consider the years of many generations."

The farmers say there is "no real money in it" but sugar-making comes at a time when ordinary farm work is slack ... the spring makes them restless and they want to get into the woods and see the sap running.

MAPLE POPCORN

2 cups sugar — ½ cup maple syrup
1½ cups water — 1 tsp. vinegar
½ tsp. salt — 1 tsp. maple flavouring
5 quarts popped corn

Butter the sides of large saucepan. Combine sugar, salt, syrup, vinegar and water. Cook until hard ball stage, then stir in maple flavouring. Slowly pour mixture over the popped corn, mixing gently. Butter hands and shape into small balls.

MAPLE NUTS

1 cup flour — 2 cups rye meal
⅓ cup corn meal — 1 egg — salt
½ cup maple syrup — 1⅛ c. water
3 tsp. baking powder

Combine dry ingredients in bowl.
Beat egg and add to maple syrup
and 1 cup cold water. Mix all
well.
Cut batter into small dabs and
fry in hot fat. Cook to a
maple brown — a mouth-
watering "doughnut" of maple
sweetness.

188

MAPLE FOG

Scald 1½ cups milk in top of double boiler.

2 eggs, separated ⌐ 1 Tbsp. gelatine
¼ cup cold water — 1 cup maple syrup
⅛ tsp. salt ⌐ ½ tsp. vanilla

Beat egg yolks, combine with a bit of the hot milk. Blend with yolks, cook about 4 minutes.
Soak gelatine in cold water and then add to hot milk mixture.
Add MAPLE SYRUP and salt and blend well. Chill. Gently fold in stiffly beaten egg whites and vanilla.
Chill.
Serve with Fluffy Sauce
(see p. 149)

"The lower you tap the more the sap"

"The older the tree the sweeter the sap"

"Trees differ for sugar as cows
   do for milk"

"Trees by the brook or spring
   run much sap"

Sap Sayings

189

Cumberland Maple Pie

Prepare a baked pastry shell.
2 cups MAPLE Syrup — 2 tbsp. flour
½ cup milk — ½ cup light cream
1 Tbsp. butter

Mix MAPLE Syrup and flour in a saucepan, then add milk, cream and butter. Stir gently over moderate heat and boil to 210°. Cool, then pour into shell. (For a change you can cover with a top crust). Bake low in the oven at 375° (preheated) about 30-40 minutes or until golden brown.

Maple Cream Topping

1 cup whipping cream
½ cup MAPLE SYRUP.
Cream must be COLD. Whip until begins to thicken. Add syrup and beat until it retains its shape. Serve with cake, pudding or custard.

Rice Pudding

1 cup MAPLE SYRUP — 3 eggs
2-1/2 cup boiled rice — 1/2 tsp. salt
2-1/2 cup milk — 1/2 tsp. nutmeg
1 cup raisins

Combine. Place in buttered baking dish. Bake until firm (at about 325°). Serve hot or cold, with or without cream.   Serves 8

New Hampshire Pudding

2 cups milk — 1 cup MAPLE SYRUP
3 tbsp. minute Tapioca — Dash Salt

Cook in double boiler about 15 minutes. Add beaten yolk of 2 eggs, then fold in beaten whites. Serve in sherbert glasses topped with one Tablespoon whipped cream. Serves 6.

MAPLE EGGNOG

12 eggs, separated ﹂ ½ cup bourbon
½ cup maple sugar ﹂ ¾ cup rum
4 cups cold milk ﹂ Ground nutmeg
2 cups whipping cream ﹁ dash salt

Beat egg yolks and gradually
add the maple sugar. Beat well.
Add milk, bourbon, rum and salt.
Whip the cream. Beat egg whites
till peaks are stiff. Combine
yolks, whites and whipped
cream. Serve immediately
in large punch bowl, adding a
few drops of maple flavouring
just before serving.

HINTS:

MAPLE SUGAR or Maple Syrup
taste heavenly with a dish of
old fashioned — or pre cooked —
OATMEAL PORRIDGE.

Montreal Omelet

3 Tbsp. MAPLE SYRUP
5 eggs, separated — butter
½ cup fine almond slices
½ tsp. vanilla

Add syrup to well beaten egg yolks.
Then add vanilla and pinch of salt.
Beat egg whites to dry peaks and
gently fold into yolk mixture.

Use medium size frying pan with
enough butter - cover with almonds
and immediately add egg mixture.
Cook slowly — about 6 minutes.
Then place in moderate oven for
about 8-10 minutes.

Serve folded or flat, with warm
MAPLE SYRUP

MAPLE SUCRERIE PIE

Prepare your favourite pastry shell
and bake 10 minutes at 400°F.
Prick the bottom lightly. For a change
here is a pastry used in Quebec
country homes:

    ¼ cup butter - ½ cup shortening
    1½ cups whole-wheat flour
    1 Tbsp. sugar and dab of cold water

PIE FILLING -
1½ cups MAPLE SYRUP - ¼ cup milk
1 cup brown sugar - yolks of 4 eggs
2 Tbsp. butter - 4 egg whites, beaten

Combine and mix well the syrup,
sugar, milk, butter and egg yolks.
Carefully fold in the beaten egg
whites. Pour into shell and bake
350° for about a half hour.

For a change, sprinkle nutmeg or
your favourite spice underneath
or on top of pie filling.
Sometimes called Backwoods Pie.

Quinte Orange Surprise

Cook 6 sweet potatoes and peel.
Add 3 Tbsp. butter, ½ cup orange
juice, ½ cup maple syrup, and a
dash of salt and pepper.

Cut 6 large oranges in half.
Scoop and juice, leaving shells.

Place maple mixture in orange
shells and cook about 20 minutes
at 325°.

ELMIRA PIE
(from UpState)

1¾ cups bread flour
12 Tbsp. shortening — 1 tsp. salt

Using 2 knives, chop shortening
into flour and salt until mixture
barely hangs together. Line a
pie pan, and leave enough for
a top crust.

Fill pie with:
4 cups sliced green (or tart) apples
⅔ cups sugar — 2 Tbsp. butter
½ tsp. cinnamon — ⅓ tsp. nutmeg
Pour on top of mixture, about
⅔ cup maple syrup. (Sometimes
I use a bit more)

Cover with crust and crimp the
edges. Coat with egg white
and grated maple sugar. Bake
about 40 minutes at 375°.

This is a north country
     breakfast pie.

Liquer D'Erable

2 tasses whiskey
2 tasses sirop d'erable

Combinez whiskey et sirop d'érable
Remuez et mettez en bouteille.
Se Conserve de 1 à 2 ans au
refrigenateur.   Délicieux!

Banana Flambees

8 bananas – peeled – not too ripe
2 Tbsp. lemon juice – 2 tbsp soft butter
½ cup Maple Syrup
2 Tbsp frozen orange juice
¼ tsp. cinnamon – 4 Tbsp. Brandy

Place fruit in shallow baking dish.
Combine lemon and orange juice,
Maple Syrup and butter and pour
over bananas. Sprinkle with
cinnamon. Bake 30 mins. at 325°,
basting occasionally.
Just before serving, sprinkle with
Brandy and ignite. Serve flaming.

197

MAPLE - APPLE CHUTNEY

Combine 12 peeled, cored chopped
apples with :
3 red peppers — 2 green peppers,
1 medium onion chopped fine.
Add 1 pint cider vinegar and
simmer about 1 hour. Then add:
Juice of 4 lemons — 1 cup raisins
¼ tsp. Cayenne pepper — 1 Tbsp. salt
1 cup sugar (brown) — 1¼ cups maple sugar
1 Tbsp. ground ginger

Cook about an hour. Stir often.
Store in sterilized jars.

198

The sweet sap comes from the starch stored during the growing season. Enzymes and climate change starch to sugars. The sap contains on average – 97.5% water, 2.4% sugar, 0.1% mineral matter.

Sweet Slaw Salad

Shred a small cabbage. Add the following dressing:

2 beaten eggs ⌐ ¾ cup maple syrup
¼ cup vinegar ⌐ ⅓ tsp. dry mustard
2 Tbsp. butter ⌐ ½ cup whipped cream

Combine beaten eggs with syrup and dry ingredients, adding butter and vinegar. Stir well in a double boiler until thick. Cool a bit, then put in refrigerator to chill. Just before serving, add the whipped cream and lightly toss with the shredded cabbage.

Visit:
The Danforth Collection (New England Maple Museum) – maple sugaring artifacts –

199

"There is on it an excellent Maple Sucrerie, capable of producing annually from 300 to 600 pounds of Sugar." Quebec Gazette, 1780

SUCRE A LA CREME

1 lb. granulated Maple Sugar
1 pt. whipping cream — 2 oz. butter
½ tsp. salt

Cook sugar, cream and salt in a heavy pot until the candy thermometer registers 240°F. Quickly pour it into a bowl to prevent further cooking and add the butter. Beat and beat with a wooden spoon until the mixture becomes heavy and sugary, but is easily poured into a foil pan which you put into the frig. to harden.

from collection of
les Producteurs de Sucre d'érable
du Quebec

MAPLE MOON MAGIC
(Punch)

1 cup maple syrup — 1 cup orange juice
½ cup each - brandy and lemon juice
½ cup maraschino cherry syrup
1 orange — thinly sliced
1 lemon — thinly sliced
1 lime — thinly sliced
Optional - 1 bottle (⅘ qt.) Champagne

Combine syrup, juices, brandy and
cherry syrup. Stir well and
allow to stand about an hour.
Chill. Just before serving add
champagne and pour over ice
in a punch bowl. Garnish with
fruit slices.

With champagne - about 8 cups
Without champagne - about 3½ cups

"Hear I met with a Grate meney...
that Came a Grate Distans with
thare furs, skins and Mapel
Suga."   1765

201

References

The Provincial, State and Federal Departments of Agriculture have numerous brochures, bulletins, papers and research studies that are available on request. The classic book on Maple Sugaring is the Helen and Scott Nearing 1970 Schocken **The Maple Sugar Book**. Also check the library index for numerous articles in a variety of Canadian and American magazines and newspapers. In addition here are listed a few of the older sources that I found particularly informative.

Barbeau, Marius: "Maple sugar: Its Native Origin", Transaction of the Royal Society of Canada, 1946, Vol. XL.

Blackbird, Andrew J.: **History of the Ottawa and Chippewa Indians of Michigan,** 1887, Ypsilanti Press.

Burroughs, John: **Winter Sunshine,** 1881, Houghton Mifflin; **Signs and Seasons,** 1914, Houghton Mifflin.

Collingwood, O. H.: "Maple Sugar and Syrup", 1938, N. Y. State Exp. Station.

Dana, Dorothea: **Sugar Bush,** 1947, Thomas Nelson.

de Crevecoeur, Hector St. John: **Sketches of 18th Century America,** 1925, Yale Press.

Finlay, M. C.: **Our American Maples,** 1935, Georgian.

Follett, Muriel: **A Drop in the Bucket,** 1941, Stephen Daye Press.

Herr, C. S.: "Maple Syrup and Sugar Production in New Hampshire", 1938, Univ. N. H.

McIntyre, A. C.: "Maple Industry in Pennsylvania", 1932, Pa. St. Bulletin #280.

Moodie, Susanna S.: **Roughing It in the Bush** (1852) and **Life in the Clearings** (1953), Toronto.

Rogers, Julia E.: **The Tree Book,** 1935, Doubleday, Doran & Co.

Rush, Benjamin: **An Account of the Sugar Maple-Tree of the U. S.,** 1792, Aiken.

Schoolcraft, Henry P.: **History, Condition and Prospects of the Indian Tribes of the U. S.,** 1884, Lippincott, J. B.

Smith, W. L.: **The Pioneers of Old Ontario,** 1923, Morang.

Spencer, J. B .: **Maple Sugar Industry in Canada,** 1913, Ottawa.

Strickland, Samuel: **Twenty-Seven Years in Canada West,** 1853, Bentley.

Traill, Catherine Parr: **The Backwoods of Canada** 1836; **The Female Emigrant's Guide** 1854; **The Canadian Settler's Guide** 1860, Stanford.

Thoreau, Henry David: **Early Spring in Massachusetts,** 1893, Houghton Mifflin.